THE WHOLE TOOTH-AND-CLAW STORY

Glenn Murphy wrote his first book, *Why Is Snot Green?*, while working at the Science Museum, London. Since then he has written around twenty popular-science titles aimed at kids and teens, including the bestselling *How Loud Can You Burp?* and *Space: The Whole Whizz-Bang Story*.

These days he lives in sunny, leafy North Carolina – with his wife Heather, his son Sean, and two *unfeasibly* large felines.

SCIENCE SORTED

YUM

PREDATORS
THE WHOLE TOOTH-AND-CLAW STORY

MIAOW!

GLENN MURPHY

Illustrated by Mike Phillips

MACMILLAN CHILDREN'S BOOKS

For the staff, volunteers and adopters of the Conservators Center, North Carolina. In recognition of tireless efforts rarely seen or appreciated, but valiantly undertaken. Here's to you, and to our beloved carnivorous critters . . .

First published 2015 by Macmillan Children's Books
an imprint of Pan Macmillan
20 New Wharf Road, London N1 9RR
Associated companies throughout the world
www.panmacmillan.com

ISBN 978-1-4472-8504-5

Text copyright © Glenn Murphy 2015
Illustrations copyright © Mike Phillips 2015

The right of Glenn Murphy and Mike Phillips to be identified as the
author and illustrator of this work has been asserted by them in accordance
with the Copyright, Designs and Patents Act 1988.

1 3 5 7 9 8 6 4 2

A CIP catalogue record for this book is available from the British Library.

Typeset by Dan Newman, Perfect Bound Ltd.
Printed and bound by CPI Group (UK) Ltd, Croydon CRO 4YY

Picture credits: All photographs Shutterstock except for the following: page 16 top, middle and bottom, reproduced
courtesy of Glenn Murphy; 17, 125, 127, 131, 132, 133, 145, 148, 150, 151 (bottom), 181, 182 (bottom), 189 (bottom),
216 reproduced courtesy of Taylor Hattori Images; 161 Andries Hoogerwerf/Wikimedia Commons. All photographs of
interviewees for the Focus features supplied and reproduced courtesy of the interviewees in question.

www.taylorhattoriimages.zenfolio.com www.facebook.com/TaylorHattoriImages

CONTENTS

Introduction   2

Prehistoric Predators   18

   Focus: The Tyrannosaur Hunter   46

Ravenous Raptors   72

   Focus: The Raptor Wrangler   92

   Focus: From Raptor Rescue to Falconry   118

Crafty Cats   120

   Focus: The Mother of Lions   144

Cunning Canines   168

   Focus: The Wolf Whisperers   179

Answers   219

INTRODUCTION

This book, as you may have gathered from the *spiffing* front cover, is all about predators.

Sweet! When do we start?

Right away! But before we go, here's a quick question to set the scene. Something for *you* to ponder. That is: what *is* a predator, and why do predators exist?

What makes a predator?

Put simply, predators are animals that hunt and eat other animals. This can take quite a bit of effort to accomplish. But compared to plant-munching herbivores, they eat less and rest more. And believe it or not, predators also help their prey to survive!

Aren't ALL animals predators, then?

Nope. There are plenty of other ways for an

animal to make a living besides being a predator.

Some eat **plants** or **fungi** instead. We call those **herbivores** and **fungivores**.

Some eat dead **animals**, but don't actually hunt or kill things themselves. We call those **scavengers**, or **carrion-eaters**. And less picky **omnivores** eat plants *and* animals — dead or alive.

So what makes predators special?

True **predators** live entirely (or almost entirely) on living things that they hunt for themselves, otherwise known as **prey**.

At this point, it might be worth asking: why do animals eat each other at all? Why aren't they all happy, peaceful herbivores, like sheep, cows and elephants?

Errr ... because animals are tasty and nutritious?

That's a big part of it, yes. It takes a *lot* of plant protein to build a **sheep**, and even *more* to build an **elephant**. So plant-munching herbivores generally have to eat all day, just to maintain their bodies.

But by snacking on meaty, herbivore **muscles**, lions and wolves get to eat several **months'** worth of stored protein *all at once*. This saves them having to graze all day, and allows them to **fast** (or stop eating) once in a while. Which is a handy trick when your food becomes scarce.

So herbivores are like predator pantries?

You could say that, yes. Or four-legged, meat-filled fridges!

That might not sound very fair to the herbivores. But believe it or not, predators also *help* prey species to **survive**.

Eh? They help animals to survive by eating them? That doesn't make any sense . . .

If they ate *all* the available prey animals, then no — it wouldn't. But predators very rarely do this. Instead, they only pick off a few at a time. Usually the **smallest**, **slowest**, **weakest** or **worst adapted**. The rest of the prey animals are left to live, grow, and multiply.

Over time, this removes small, slow, weak or poorly adapted animals from the landscape, leaving mostly strong, fit, healthy animals behind.

Wow. Never thought of it like that.

What's more, over long periods of time, prey animals change — gaining features like **horns**, **teeth**, **tusks** and **camouflaged coat patterns**.

If these changes help prey animals to survive predator attacks, then they may split and develop into new species, that look nothing like each other.

In this way, predators drive the **evolution** of prey animals, and increase the number of different animal **species** on the planet! Without predators, prey animals would have little reason to change, and there would be far fewer species around.

Which, if nothing else, would make a trip to the zoo a pretty boring day out.

How many kinds of predators are there?

In short, **lots**. In fact, there are almost as many predators as there are living things to eat. If it swims, crawls, trots or scampers, then somewhere out there there's an animal that hunts it.

Really? You get tiny predators as well as big ones?

Yep. Though we won't be looking at all of them in this book, the world of predators includes all creatures, great and small.

Tiny land predators include **spiders**, **scorpions**, **centipedes** and some species of **ant**, **beetle** and **snail**.

In our oceans, lakes and rivers, **aquatic predators** include **arrow worms**, **starfish**, **jellyfish**, **squid**, **octopus** and many types of **fish**.

Of course, small predators are also prey for larger, **intermediate predators** such as **geckos**, **shrews** and **swifts** (on land) and **groupers**, **seals** and **penguins** (at sea).

In turn, these guys are prey for even *larger* **super-predators** like **foxes**, **badgers**, **hawks**, **pythons**, **pumas**, **killer whales** and **Komodo dragons**.

Super-predators

Intermediate predators

Small predators

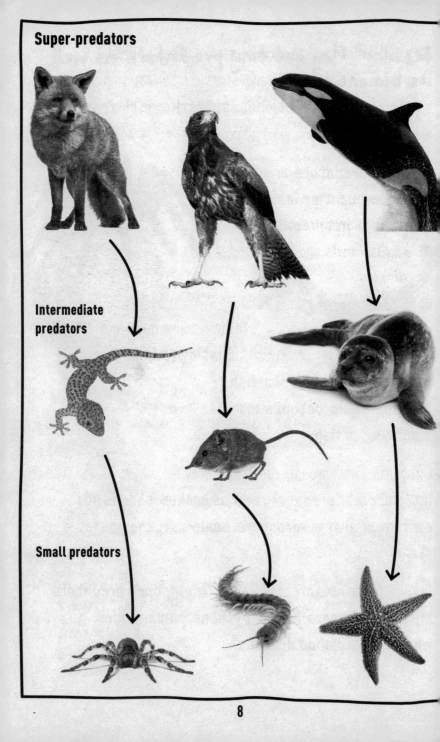

As a matter of fact, there are *so* many types of predator that it's hard to know where to start! So to keep things simple – this book will be looking at four groups of predators in particular.

These are:

- **dinosaurs** and other **prehistoric predators**
- **eagles**, **owls** and other **birds of prey**
- **lions**, **tigers** and their whiskery **cat-like** relatives
- **foxes**, **wolves** and other **dog-like** hunters.

Besides humans, that is. We humans are ever-present, and armed with our tools and technologies, we're dangerous to all of the world's wildlife. More on that later . . .

In short, we're looking at **apex predators**. These are dedicated meat-eaters with no natural predators of their own. Big, important animals that affect their prey and their environment in big, obvious ways.

So where did all these predators come from?

Good question. Like all other animals, predators have their origins in tiny bacteria that oozed from the oceans billions of years ago. Eventually, these bugs fused and evolved into thousands of wonderful body-shapes. Some of these survived to become predatory, prehistoric animals. But many were lost forever to the sands of time.

Wait – all animals came from the SAME place and time?

The same **place**, yes. But different animals evolved at different **times**.

So which came first?

Well, the Earth is around 4.6 billion years old. And for the first billion years, there was **no** life at all. Then, around **three and a half billion years** ago, the first, ancient **bacteria** formed.

These simple, single-celled creatures were little more than a circle of DNA surrounded by a fatty bubble. For the most part, they just sat on rocks, drifted around in the oceans, absorbed things, and multiplied. For the next three billion years, that's pretty much all our planet had to offer.

Then around **600 million years ago**, these single-celled creatures evolved tiny tentacles and propellers, and began to move themselves around in search of food.

Also known as protists. Protozoa means 'first animals' in Greek.

These early **protozoa** oozed and buzzed everywhere on the planet, and are still all around us today (though without a microscope, they're too small to see). Since they often 'ate' (or absorbed) each other, you *could* say that these were the world's first predators.

But they weren't really animals, right?

No, they weren't. Animal bodies contain more than one living cell — usually **millions** of **billions** of them, all working together. It took another **100 million years** or so before single-celled bacteria and protists began sticking together and cooperating. In doing so, they evolved into slimy **plants** and **fungi**, such as **algae**, **slime moulds** and **lichens**. They also formed the world's first multi-celled **animals**.

At first, these were simple, non-moving sea creatures like **sponges** and **sea cucumbers**. Later, around **500 million years ago**, came predatory **worms**, **anemones** and **jellyfish**. Then around **400 million years** ago things got *really* interesting . . .

Why's that? What happened then?

The continents shifted and mountains were raised, creating warm, shallow seas where animal life could more easily develop. Some soft-bodied animals evolved chalky **shells** and **armour-plating** to avoid being eaten by predators. Soon, these snail-like **molluscs** and lobster-like **arthropods** were everywhere.

Meanwhile a few, wormy sea animals were developing **stiff notocords** and **backbones**, paving the way for **vertebrates** with bony skeletons.

In other words, there was an *explosion* of animal body shapes. During this one 100-million-year period, animal life went from 'simple and squishy' to 'weird, wonderful and complex'. Scientists call this period the **Cambrian explosion**.

Crazy. So what happened after that?

After the Cambrian period came the **Devonian period**. And by the end of *that*, around 350 million years ago, strange, armour-plated fish were swimming in the oceans, and four-legged **tetrapods** were crawling out of the seas and on to the land.

These bony amphibians looked like giant **newts** or **salamanders**. The one-metre-long tetrapod *Acanthostega* lived in shallow rivers, and used its stubby legs to paddle, rather than walk. But the 1.5-metre *Icthyostega* had several stout toes on each foot, and probably pulled itself over land, between ponds and rivers.

13

These animals — or other tetrapods like them — were the ancestors of *all* the land predators that followed.

Like crocodiles and dinosaurs?

Eventually, yes. But not before a major disaster almost killed everything on the planet . . .

Like what – an asteroid?

Nope. A **volcano**. Or more likely, a *supervolcano*.

Around **250 million years ago**, there were massive volcanic eruptions in what would *now* be called Siberia. Superheated ash and poisonous sulphur dioxide spewed into the atmosphere, blanketing the land.

Back then, most of the continents were still stuck together into a single **supercontinent** called **Pangaea**, so for most land-based plants and animals, there was little chance of escape.

14

It was terrible. Over **90 per cent of all species** on the planet were destroyed, including **50 per cent** of all **plants**, **96 per cent** of all **insects** and **arthropods**, and at least **two-thirds** of all land-based **amphibians** and **reptiles**. Scientists call this massive die-off the **Permian Mass Extinction**.

Yikes! So what DID survive?

In the oceans, the remaining fish and arthropods regrouped and began evolving anew. On land, ferns, seed plants and insects began to regroup, too. But perhaps most importantly (at least for this book!) the disappearance of almost *all* the large reptiles cleared the slate for a whole new generation of predatory animals, including **dinosaurs**, **birds** and (eventually) **mammals**. **Predators** that would dominate the remainder of our planet's history. And **predators** we will be looking at in more detail here.

Know Your Stuff: Animal Families

Before we go any further, it'll be helpful to know how scientists talk about predators, and sort them into animal families and classes. In everyday life, we use **class names** (2S, 4B, 5C) and **family names** (Smith, Campbell, O'Neill) to help **separate** and **group** people. For example, we know all the kids in class 2B are in Year 2, but have a different timetable to class 2C.

Glenn **Murphy**, Heath **Murphy** and Frank **Murphy** are all related, but they're **different people**, with **different ages** (currently **39**, **44**, and **72**!)

For over 300 years, scientists have been grouping animals, plants and other life-forms into separate classes and families, too. This makes it easier to compare and study them in detail. The first person to have a serious crack at this was Swedish zoologist **Carolus Linnaeus**. Or Carl, to his mates.

Linnaeus named and classified over 11,000 species of plants and animals, and in 1735 published them in his book *Systema Naturae* (Natural Systems).

His nifty system used four groups or categories of life. These were:

Class • Order • Genus • Species

Here, *order* means 'rank', while *genus* means 'race', and *species* means 'form'. Here's how Linnaeus would have classified your pet cat:

Assuming, that is, you have a standard, domestic kitty-cat at home, and not a tiger or leopard or something. You never know. Some people do . . .

Class: *Mammalia*
Order: *Carnivora* (toothy, clawed carnivore)
Genus: *Felis* (feline, or cat-like)
Species: *domesticus* (domesticated, or tame)

Right away, this handy grouping system tells us all kinds of things about the animal.

First, your kitty-cat belongs to a **Class** of hairy, milk-producing animals called **mammals**. This makes her quite different to, say, an alligator (Class **Reptilia**) or newt (Class **Amphibia**) – neither of which have hair *or* milk.

Second, she's in the order of mammals known as **Carnivora**. This means she's a carnivore, that she eats meat or fish (at least some of the time), and she probably has sharp, pointy teeth for ripping at tasty flesh. This separates her from **rabbits** (Order **Lagomorpha**) and **two-toed sloths** (Order **Xenartha**), neither of which (thankfully) have scary, flesh-ripping teeth.

Third, she's a **feline** (cat-like) animal with a flattened nose, retractable claws, and other features unique to cats, small and large. This separates her from **canine** (dog-like) **wolves** and **foxes** (Genus **Canis**), which have long snouts, and cannot retract their claws.

Fourth, she's a **tame** or **domestic cat**. This means she probably weighs no more than 10 kilograms and lives with humans that feed and look after her.

PREHISTORIC PREDATORS

Were dinosaurs just big, meat-eating lizards?

Not quite. They weren't lizards, they didn't all eat meat, and many weren't so big. Dinosaurs were a huge, varied group of reptiles. Some were predatory meat-eaters, others were peaceful plant-eaters, and they ranged in size from tiny to immense.

But there were big reptiles creeping about long before the dinosaurs came along, right?

Right. Chunky reptiles hit the scene around 50 million years earlier.

So what's the difference? Were the dinosaurs just bigger?

Not all of them, no. Some dinosaurs were little larger than chickens or pigeons. Others grew to the size of fire engines. Since so few of them were fossilized, it's hard to know how big the 'average' dinosaur was. But in any case, size isn't really what separates dinosaurs from other reptiles.

FOWL PLAY!

So what DOES separate them?

For one thing, dinosaurs walked with their knees and feet right beneath their bodies.

Crocodiles and alligators walk with their legs splayed out to their sides. So do other leggy reptiles like lizards, tortoises and turtles. This gives them a creepy, crawly, side-to-side walking style. Most prehistoric reptiles walked the same way.

Snakes, of course, have no legs at all, so they slither, rather than crawl. Extra creepy.

But dinosaurs were different. Dinosaurs held their legs vertically, and kept their knees and feet *under* their hips when they walked. This lifted their bellies high off the ground and allowed them to walk, trot and even *run* the way mammals do.

19

So dinosaurs moved more like cats and dogs than crocodiles?

Yes. The big, slow ones moved more like **rhinos** and **elephants**, while the faster ones (including pretty much all of the predators) moved more like **ostriches**.

Why is that?

It all depends on the shape of the hips. Over a century ago, early dino-scientists separated dinosaurs into two main groups, based on their differing hip-shapes.

In all leggy animals (amphibians, reptiles, birds and mammals), the hip bone is also known as the **pelvis**. But one **pelvis** is actually *three* bones held tightly together — the **ilium**, the **ischium** and the **pubis**.

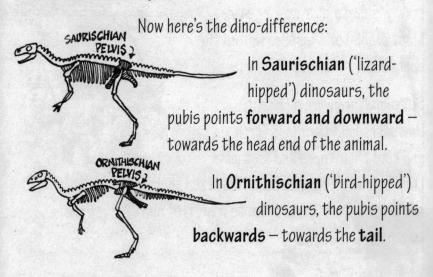

Now here's the dino-difference:

SAURISCHIAN PELVIS

In **Saurischian** ('lizard-hipped') dinosaurs, the pubis points **forward and downward** — towards the head end of the animal.

ORNITHISCHIAN PELVIS

In **Ornithischian** ('bird-hipped') dinosaurs, the pubis points **backwards** — towards the **tail**.

Saurischian (lizard–hipped) dinosaurs included:

■ Four-legged dinosaurs, such as the immense, **plant-eating** *Apatosaurus*, *Brachiosaurus*, *Camarasaurus* and *Diplodocus*.

■ Two-legged, small, **meat-eating predators** like *Deinonychosaurus*, *Ornithomimus* and *Velociraptor*.

■ **Larger predators** such as the awesome *Ceratosaurus*, *Carnosaurus*, *Spinosaurus* and *Tyrannosaurus*.

Ornithischian (bird–hipped) dinosaurs included:

■ Huge, **armour-plated herbivores**, like *Stegosaurus*, *Ankylosaurus* and *Edmontonia*.

■ Large, **herding herbivores**, like *Iguanodon*, *Hadrosaurus* and *Hypsilophodon*.

■ **Thick-headed, plant-munching** *Pachycephalosaurs*.

■ Rhino-like, herbivorous **Ceratopsians** with frilled or horned heads, such as *Pachyrhinosaurus*, *Triceratops* and *Pentaceratops*.

So the lizard-hipped ones were predators?

Most of them, yes. With the exception of the huge, four-legged, plant-eating **Sauropods**, all the lizard-hipped dinosaurs ate meat.

So which came first – the meat-munchers or the plant-munchers?

I'm glad you asked. We're coming to that next . . .

What did the very first dinosaur look like?

The first dinosaurs appeared between 250 and 200 million years ago. They were smallish, meat-eating hunters — a bit like a miniature Tyrannosaurus rex.

The first dinos were MINI-REXES? Sweet!

Well, not *every* animal gets fossilized and found by scientists.

We'll look at why fossils are so rare the next section — so hang in there!

So we can't know for sure whether we might one day find another, older, dinosaur fossil. For now, the oldest dinosaur fossils we have date back 230 million years.

Herrerasaurus and *Eoraptor* were both found in the rocky mountains of Argentina. *Eoraptor* was cat-sized, while *Herrerasaurus* was closer to horse-sized. They were both two-legged carnivores that hunted smaller prey.

As far as we can tell, they — or something like them — were the first true dinosaurs to walk the Earth.

So the two-legged dinos came first, and four-legged ones came later?

Yes, *much* later. The period that followed saw the rise of more reptiles. These included:

- the first **snakes** and **lizards**
- early **crocodiles** and **alligators**
- strange, reptilian sea monsters
- the first flying reptiles, and
- two **new orders of reptiles** with **flexible ankles** and **grasping hands**.

Let me guess – dinosaurs, right?

Right. The lizard-hipped and bird-hipped **dinosaurs**.

So what came after those?

A little later came the **plant-munching sauropodomorphs**. These herbivores developed long necks for grazing on high tree branches, and eventually became so bulky that they had to stand on all fours, like outsized giraffes or elephants.

Later, these evolved into even bigger dinosaurs like *Brachiosaurus* and *Diplodocus*. Animals *so* large that few predators could ever hope to attack them.

What about Stegosauruses and Triceratops . . . es?

As far as we know, *Stegosaurus* didn't arrive until around **175 million years ago** – 55 million years after *Eoraptor*. As for *Triceratops*, she didn't show up until about **68 million years ago**. That was **162 million years** after *Eoraptor*.

In other words, *Triceratops* lived closer in time to us than it did to the earliest known dinosaur!

Eoraptor — 162 million years — Homo sapiens — 68 million years

Crazy! So if the earliest dinosaurs were predators, and the plant-munchers weren't around yet, then what did they eat?

They preyed on the many other reptiles that walked, crawled and scampered across the Earth. There were plenty of other **non**-dinosaurs to munch on . . .

Triassic Park

Dinosaurs first evolved during the Triassic period (250–200 million years ago). But they weren't the only reptiles around. Here's a short list of other animals that shared their world:

- **Parasuchians** – Freshwater fish-eaters that looked much like *gharials* – the skinny-snouted freshwater crocs of modern India.

- **Sphenosuchians** – Ancestors of modern crocodiles, with long, skinny legs. Like a cross between a crocodile and a greyhound.

ON YOUR MARKS...

- **Aetosaurs** – Stocky, four-legged plant-munchers with spikes and heavy armour-plating.

- **Rauischians** – Massive, meat-eating predators. Some walked on two legs, others on all fours.

- **Pterosaurs** – Chicken-sized reptiles that flapped and glided on bat-like wings. Larger *pterodactyls* came later.

- **Dicynodonts** – Beaky, bow-legged reptiles. The larger ones looked like a cross between a rhino and a turtle!

- **Cynodonts** – Long-snouted, mammal-like cousins of the dicynodonts (described above).

- **Dinosauromorphs** – Reptilian forerunners of the dinosaurs that walked with legs beneath their bodies, but lacked grasping hands.

- **Early Dinosaurs** – These looked like smaller, skinnier *T. rexes*. Later, the first four-legged, plant-eating dinosaurs appeared.

How do we know what dinosaurs ate?

Almost all of our knowledge comes from fossils. Fossilized skeletons tell us what dinosaurs looked like and fossilized teeth, claws and poo can tell us what they ate.

What exactly IS a fossil? Is it just a really old skeleton or shell buried in the ground?

Not quite. Bones and shells break down (or **decompose**) slowly, but not that slowly. Within 50 years, an entire **elephant** or **whale skeleton** will be completely dissolved. **Human skeletons** take less than 20 years to break down. Unless, that is, you preserve them with special embalming fluids, and bury them inside a protective sarcophagus or coffin.

Most dinosaur species died out more than 50 *million* years ago. With no one around to mummify them or build dino-sized coffins, there's no way a dinosaur skeleton could survive that long in loose soil. So a fossil is a bit more than that.

WAAAAAAAAAAA

What ARE they, then?

Fossils are traces or remains of living things **preserved inside rocks**. For the most part, soft, squishy things (like bacteria and jellyfish) do not fossilize at all.

Things with shells or bones (like limpets, turtles and tyrannosaurs) have a much better chance. But even *they* don't fossilize often.

Why's that?

Boneless things with soft, juicy bodies are usually eaten by scavengers or bacteria long before they can be buried and fossilized.

Animals with skeletons get eaten too, of course. But their tough, indigestible bones are often licked clean and left behind.

As we'll see later on, some predators – like owls and hyenas – eat bones, too. But most do not.

Sometimes, entire skeletons are buried intact, with all the bones still in the right places. Palaeontologists *love* finding these. But sadly, that doesn't happen as often as they would like.

Why not? Dinosaurs were bony, right? So there should be dinosaur fossils buried EVERYWHERE, right?

Because in order to survive for millions of years, even **bony** bodies must be encased in **rock**. And not just *any* rock, either. A special type of rock called **sedimentary rock**.

Sedimentary rocks are formed as bits of existing rock are broken off and shifted around by wind or water. This creates layers of sediment that collect at the base of a mountain, the foot of a cliff, or the bottom of a lake or ocean.

So then what happens?

As the layers of sediment build up and water flows through them, they become cemented together, forming one, huge layer of rock. Sand layers form **sandstone**. Silt layers form **siltstone**. Mud layers form **mudstone**, and so on.

These are the types of rocks you usually find fossils in. When fresh bodies are buried by mudslides, washed into rivers and watering holes, or sucked into sticky sands and bogs, then they *might* be preserved within the sediment layers before they have time to decompose, and may *just* survive the transformation of those layers into sedimentary rock.

Hooray!

But you don't find sedimentary rocks just *anywhere*. Only certain spots on the planet will be forming sedimentary rocks at any given time. This explains why you don't find fossils all over the place.

This also explains why there are so many species 'missing' from the fossil record. Only a *fraction* of the animals that ever lived (dinosaurs included) have been lucky enough to fossilize.

That said, you'd be surprised at some of the things scientists *have* found. And at how much we've learned from them.

Like what?

In 1974, scientists found **thousands** of *Coelophysis* skeletons buried together at the **Ghost Ranch** site in New Mexico. This one find proved that these particular dinosaurs moved in **herds** or **packs**.

In 1975, American palaeontologist **Jack Horner** found baby, juvenile and adult *Maiasaura* fossils buried together in one, huge **nesting site**. This proved that at least *some* dinosaurs **reared their young**. (Most other reptiles abandon their young after hatching.)

And in 1997, palaeontologists in China found **dozens** of *Sinosauropteryx* and *Sinornithosaurus* fossils. These 'dino-bird' fossils showed traces of hair-like **feathers**.

This not only backed up the long-held theory that **some dinosaurs evolved into birds**. It also suggests that this happened **much earlier** than we thought!

Wow! Dino-herds and dino-birds! Cool!

That's not all. Since then, we've X-rayed fossilized dinosaur **eggs** – revealing fully preserved **embryos** inside, telling us how baby dinosaurs developed. And we've analysed fossilized **dinosaur poo** (or **coprolite**) to find out what kinds of plants (or animals) each dinosaur ate. We've

even found trails of fossilized **dinosaur footprints**, which tell us how dino-predators **moved** and **hunted**.

Dinosaur scientists are like police detectives, looking at 70 million years of evidence to figure out 'whodunnit', and how.

Hooray for Sherlock Bones!

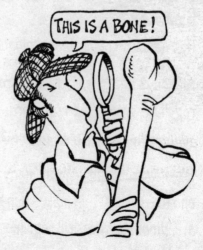

THIS IS A BONE!

How do dinosaurs get their names?

Often, dino names describe special features – like claws, horns, or armour-plating. Sometimes, we name them after the place where they are first discovered. And sometimes, we just get silly!

So most dinos are named for what they look like?

Triceratops means three-horned.

At least some part of each dinosaur's name usually refers to something that makes that family or species unique.

But don't they all look like, well . . . big lizards?

Not according to palaeontologists!

Although it's true that the word *dinosaur* means 'terrible reptile' – from the Greek words *deinos* (meaning 'terrible') and *sauros* (meaning 'lizard' or 'reptile').

It's *also* true that a great many dinosaurs have names that end in *–saurus*. This makes sense, since whatever else they are, dinosaurs *are* still reptiles.

So what do 'Velociraptor' and 'Tyrannosaurus' mean?

Those two are actually named for their behaviour, rather than their appearance.

Raptor means 'hunter' or 'thief'. Hence, we have *Velociraptor*, 'speedy hunter'. As for *Tyrannosaurs*, their family name means 'tyrant reptile', *tyrant* being a French (and English) word meaning 'absolute ruler'.

So are dinosaurs named after people and places, too?

Due to the naming rules, dino-discoverers rarely get to name dinosaurs after *themselves*. But a few have been named after famous people such as *Crichtonosaurus*, named after *Jurassic Park* author Michael Crichton.

Sometimes, though, palaeontologists just go nuts and name their precious dino-finds whatever they want. Check out the Top Ten Strange Dinosaur Names below, and be prepared to giggle . . .

Top Ten Strange Dinosaur Names

■ **Xenotarsosaurus** 'strange-ankle reptile'.

■ **Mirischia** 'wonderful pelvis'.

■ **Rugops** 'rough-face'.

■ **Enigmosaurus** 'enigmatic reptile' (the dinosaur Mona Lisa?).

■ **Alectrosaurus** 'mateless reptile' (this seems rather sad).

■ **Gasosaurus** 'gas reptile' (wouldn't want to be downwind of this guy. I wouldn't be surprised if he didn't have any mates, either).

■ **Nodosaurus** 'lumpy reptile'.

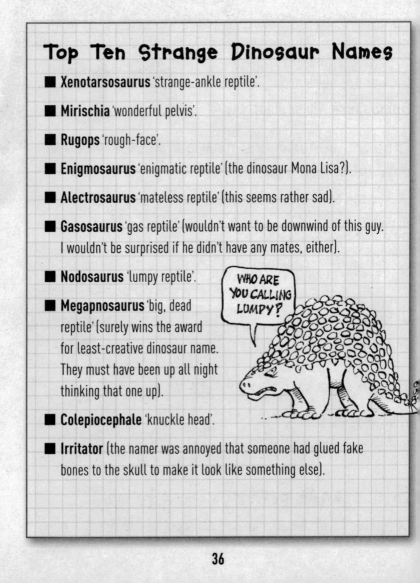

WHO ARE YOU CALLING LUMPY?

■ **Megapnosaurus** 'big, dead reptile' (surely wins the award for least-creative dinosaur name. They must have been up all night thinking that one up).

■ **Colepiocephale** 'knuckle head'.

■ **Irritator** (the namer was annoyed that someone had glued fake bones to the skull to make it look like something else).

What was the biggest, baddest dinosaur of all time?

The biggest dinosaurs were lumbering plant-eaters. But the baddest of all time were probably the **Carnosaurs** and **Spinosaurs**. These giant, two-legged predators ruled the land, long before the first Tyrannosaur arrived.

So T. rex wasn't the deadliest predator ever?

Tyrannosaurus rex was certainly very deadly. But he wasn't the *only* giant predator of the prehistoric age. Large **two-legged dinosaurs** thrived over 100 million years before *T. rex* arrived on the scene.

Really? What did THEY look like?

Well, they were fairly small. Most of them were no larger than badgers, and the largest no larger than a grizzly bear.

Still sounds pretty scary to me . . .

Compared to what came later, they were teddy bears!

By the **early Jurassic** period, which began around **200 million** years ago, predators such as *Coelophysis* were fairly common.

Coelophysis had a large brain (well, for a dinosaur at least), a mouthful of sharp, serrated teeth, and long, slender legs for running.

At three to four metres in height, it looked something like a tall, toothy ostrich. Only instead of wings, it had a pair of long, grasping arms with four hook-like talons on each hand.

They would use these to hook and slash their victims, and to hold them steady while they delivered ripping, suffocating bites with their jaws.

A few grew to sizes of six metres or more. They were probably the scariest of their kind. But the biggest and baddest were yet to come.

Yikes! Scarier than THOSE?

Yep. Around 180 million years ago came the beefier **Ceratosaurs** and **Megalosaurs**.

Ceratosaurs ('horned reptiles') grew up to seven metres long, and had three rhino-like horns — one on its snout, and one above each eye.

Megalosaurs were short-armed, two-legged predators of similar size, which prowled prehistoric Europe — where England would be today!

By 120 million years ago, the terrifying **Carnosaurs** joined the fray. These stubby-armed, three-clawed forerunners of the Tyrannosaurs included the six-metre *Fukuiraptor* (found in Japan) and the seven-metre *Siamotyrannus* (found in Thailand, formerly known as Siam).

The most common type of Jurassic carnivore, though, were **Allosaurs**. These grew up to seven and a half metres long, had enormously powerful jaws and claws, and are known to have fed on *enormous* herbivores.

They DO sound pretty nasty. So when did the Tyrannosaurs come along?

The first, primitive *Tyrannosaurs* evolved about 150 million years ago and were no bigger than sheep. The *really* big ones didn't come along until at least another 50 million years later.

These *Tyrannosaurs* grew up to **twelve metres** long (that's slightly longer than a double decker bus!) and had jaws which contained **58 massive, serrated teeth**, ideal for ripping and shredding large animal bodies.

Nicknamed 'lethal bananas' by palaeontologists, as each one was roughly banana-sized!

He MUST have been the biggest and baddest.

He was pretty big and bad, yes. But he wasn't alone. Tens of millions of years *before* the T.rex came along, the *real* bad-boys were already on the scene.

These included '*Great White Shark Reptiles*' and the *Spinosaurus* — an immense, sixteen-metre beast with a long, curved neck, clawed arms, a crocodile-like snout and a huge sail running the length of its spine.

Though they lived at least 30 million years before the *Tyrannosaurus* — had they ever met, they could have given him a real problem in a straight-up scrap!

So what did all these bad-boys eat?

Spinosaurus, for example, had a long, crocodile-like snout, ideal for eating huge fish and aquatic reptiles. Other large dino-predators preyed on small-to-medium-sized herbivores.

Some really big *Carnosaurs* and *Tyrannosaurs* may also have hunted huge, four-legged dinosaurs like *Diplodocus*.

There's also evidence that some giant predators attacked and killed *each other*, and occasionally ate their *own species* — making them dino-cannibals.

Yikes! As if they weren't scary enough!

41

Did T. rex hunt like a lion, or like a vulture?

There is little doubt that *Tyrannosaurus rex* was a fierce predator. But like lions and wolves, he probably scavenged a good part of his diet, too.

So which was he? A predator or scavenger?

It's hard to know for sure. Obviously, biologists can't study a wild *T. rex* in action, the way we do lions and vultures. As with other long-extinct animals, most of our information comes from looking at the shape of their fossilized skulls, teeth and bodies, and trying to deduce how they *might* have used them when alive.

The first *T. rex* skull was unearthed in 1902 and named *Tyrannosaurus rex* by palaeontologist Henry Osborn three years later. To Osborn, it seemed obvious that his 'king of tyrant reptiles' was a predator. After all, with those long legs, sharp claws, and rows of razor-sharp teeth, it was practically a shark on legs. What *else* could it be?

Right?

But in 1917, Canadian palaeontologist Lawrence Lambe found another *T. rex* skull, and noted that its teeth were pristine, unchipped, and seemingly free of wear and tear.

This is not what you would expect from an animal that rips and shreds at moving prey with its face. Lions, wolves, and other predators are *always* chipping and losing teeth this way.

Based on this, Lambe concluded that *T. rex* **nibbled** and **gnawed** at dead things more often than it snapped at live ones. In other words, for all his fearsome appearance, *T. rex* was a probably a **scavenger**, rather than a **hunter**.

So who was right?

Well, in the hundred years since, over **fifty** *Tyrannosaur* skeletons have been found. And after a century studying these and other specimens, we *still* can't decide!

Why not?

It's not as easy as you might think, and palaeontologists have weighed in on both sides of the argument.

Stubby little T-rex arms

The 'scavenger' team have argued that *T. rex*'s **stubby arms** would have been **useless** for grasping struggling prey, and that he was probably **too slow and clumsy** to catch them in the first place.

The 'predator' team argue that *T. rex*'s arms were short, but **powerful**. And that based on its weight and body structure, he might have hit at least **30 miles per hour at full sprint**. Not exactly cheetah speed! But still faster than most of the things it hunted.

Is there any way of KNOWING for sure?

Since predators and prey never drop dead and fossilize mid-chase, we may never find a **whole-body fossil** that settles the argument. But evidence from **trace fossils** – like **bite marks** and **footprints** – points towards the predator camp.

Bit of a riddle, isn't it?

The simple answer is, *T. rex* probably did a little of *both* — hunting whenever he saw the opportunity, but scavenging whenever it was more convenient.

But unless he scavenged more than he killed, this *still* makes *T. rex* a predator, at heart.

I s'pose...

One thing we *do* know is that *T. rex* was more like a leopard or a tiger than a wolf or lion. While wolves and lionesses hunt in **packs** and **prides**, tigers and leopards hunt solo. There is some evidence — from paired footprints and skeletons — that *T. rexes* travelled in family pairs.

They may even have been social animals — living in larger family groups that squabbled and communicated among themselves. But there's no evidence as yet that they **hunted** in packs. Chances are, *T. rex* was a solo ambush predator that stalked as close as he could, then gave chase to his (slowly) fleeing prey.

HMMM...

And if he found a nice chunk of *Hadrosaur* just lying around ... well, he wasn't going to let it go to waste ...

Focus: The Tyrannosaur Hunter

Mary H. Schweitzer is Professor of Marine, Earth, Atmospheric and Biological Sciences at NC State University, and Curator of Vertebrate Paleontology at the NC Museum of Natural Sciences. And from time to time, she digs up Tyrannosaurs . . .

What made you want to be a palaeontologist?

When I was five, my big brother left home for university. Before he left, he taught me how to read, and to *keep* me reading, he sent me dinosaur books. When he came home for Christmas, I told my brother (and all his friends) that I was going to be a *palaeontologist*. It took a long time, but eventually, I did!

What's the most exciting or important discovery you have made?

I would have to say the soft tissues and blood cells we found (sort of by accident) when we dissolved pieces of *T. rex* bone in the lab. Before that, no one believed 'real' tissues like this could remain in fossilized bone. I was as surprised as anyone. But the more I studied, the less surprising it seemed. It taught me never to take for granted what 'everybody knows'.

What are you working on right now?

We continue to look for cells and soft tissues in dinosaur bones as well as dinosaur skin, feathers, claws and beaks. These things shouldn't preserve, but they do. We're trying to figure out why.

You've become an expert on Tyrannosaurs. Do you think they were predators or scavengers?

Since we can't go back in time, and don't have any videos of them hunting, we will never know for sure. Either way, I would NOT want to run into a hungry T. rex, no matter how he hunted!

Could we ever bring back dinosaurs, using fossilized cells or DNA?

As a scientist, I can't say 'never'. But right now, I think there are way too many obstacles. We have not yet been able to recover even the tiniest fragment of dinosaur DNA. We don't know how their genes were arranged. And even if we had all that, then how would we grow our dinosaur? Inside a bird or crocodile egg? Sadly, neither one would work. And if it *did* hatch . . . well, the world is a very different place today. It's colder, there's less carbon dioxide, there are different plants and animals. And T. rex didn't evolve to eat cows . . .

BLAHHH!

Are ducks really dinosaurs?

They are! Ducks — and all other modern birds — evolved from feathery two-legged dinosaurs. By the end of the Cretaceous period (about 70 million years ago) our feathery friends were living side-by-side with their dinosaur cousins!

What?!

Well, not *ducks*, exactly. But birds very like them.

The first **bird-like dinosaurs** evolved around the end of the Jurassic period, around **150 million years** ago. The most famous fossil find of this time, *Archaeopteryx* (meaning 'ancient wings'), had long, clawed hands jutting from each of its feathered wings, and a toothy, beak-like snout.

Eighty million (or so) years later, *Tyrannosaurs*, *Velociraptors*, **bird-like dinosaurs** and **true birds** were all living side-by-side. And *all* of these probably had feathers.

Wait! T. rexes and Velociraptors were . . . fluffy?

Maybe not all over. But they most likely had *some* fluffy feathers.

Does that mean Velociraptors and T. rexes could FLY?

Sadly, no. Feathers actually evolved long *before* flying dinosaurs and birds. They probably evolved as **winter coats** first, and much later developed into handy **flight** surfaces.

Feathers may have appeared first in tiny, Jurassic dinosaurs as hollow, hairy **barbs** that trapped a layer of **warm air** against the little dinosaur's scaly skin.

Only later did they fan out into the wide, flat **vanes** we see in 'dino-birds' like *Archaeopteryx* and **true birds** like eagles.

Besides, they were both way too heavy, and neither had wings. Though it's fun to imagine!

Tyrannosaur and *Velociraptor* feathers were probably somewhere between the two. Downy, cosy, but not capable of flight.

So could *Archaeopteryx* fly?

We don't *know* for sure whether those early 'dino-birds' climbed trees and glided between them (like **flying squirrels** do), or whether they flapped and soared like modern birds. But recent studies show that *Archaeopteryx* probably *could* do more than glide.

I don't get it? If birds evolved from dinosaurs, how could they have lived at the same time?

Just because one animal family evolves from another, that doesn't mean the original family disappears. After all, we evolved from hairier (and slightly less brainy) apes, similar to **chimpanzees**. But that doesn't mean all the chimps have disappeared. At least not yet . . .

How do we KNOW that dinosaurs and birds are related?

First, there's their **bone structure**. Compare their skeletons, and you see right away that dinosaurs and birds have similar hip structures. Plus their collarbones are joined

together in the middle. This is the wishbone you find inside a roast chicken or turkey.

Next, as we've just seen, they both have **feathers**. As far as we know, no other group of animals has evolved these besides dinosaurs and birds. This suggests one evolved from the other. And since dinosaurs evolved millions of years earlier than birds . . . bingo!

Birds and dinos also lay **eggs** the same way, and produce the same kind of **eggshell**.

In fact, experts reckon that there are over **300 features** shared by **dinosaurs** and **birds** that are seen in **no other creature**. I would say that's pretty convincing evidence.

So here's a question – if they lived at the same time, why didn't dinosaurs eat birds?

They did. Or at least, they certainly would have *tried*. After all, dinosaurs had been hunting and eating each other for hundreds of millions of years by this point, so it makes sense that they would also hunt **birds**, **eggs** and **small mammals**.

Dinosaurs ate birds AND mammals?

GRRRRR!

Yep. Although given their small size and ability to escape into the air, dinos probably had more luck munching on **bird eggs** and **hatchlings** than they did adult **birds**.

For their part, the birds and mammals ate the dinosaurs right back! Well, their *eggs*, at least. This may have been one of the reasons why birds and mammals *replaced* the larger dinosaurs during the age that followed. Though smaller as adults, young birds and mammals grew much faster than their reptilian cousins. So they could set about hunting eggs soon after hatching or birth, and multiply ... well ... like **rats**.

So there were plenty of birds and mammals around by then?

By the end of the Cretaceous period (about 70 million years ago), we already had predatory birds like **owls**, **hawks** and **eagles**.

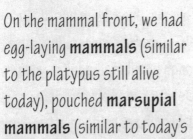

On the mammal front, we had egg-laying **mammals** (similar to the platypus still alive today), pouched **marsupial mammals** (similar to today's opossums and tree kangaroos) and a few early **rodents** and **rabbits**.

And they actually ate dinosaur eggs?

Among other things, yes.

As they do today, smaller birds and mammals would have survived mostly on **insects**, while larger birds would have eaten **fish**, **frogs**, **small reptiles**, **mammals** . . . and even the odd bit of dead **dino**!

You mean some prehistoric rat might have nibbled on a dead T. rex?

Very probably, yes.

Hmmm. I wonder what that tasted like?

OK – that's just *weird*!

What really killed the dinosaurs — asteroids, volcanoes or climate change?

Based on the latest evidence, it was probably all three. Volcanic eruptions, climate change and a huge asteroid impact *all* happened around 66 million years ago, right when most of the dinosaurs disappeared.

All three at once? How could THAT have happened?

Here's what we *do* know: a large **asteroid** or comet struck the Earth around **66 million years** ago, leaving a colossal crater in the **Yucatan** region of present day Mexico. The massive, explosive impact from this fiery extra-terrestrial death-ball would have caused deadly **tsunamis**, **earthquakes** and **wildfires** — killing everything for hundreds of miles around, and throwing **trillions** of tonnes of dirt and dust into the atmosphere.

Over the months and years that followed, that dust would have blanketed the Earth, blocking a good amount of sunlight, dropping global temperatures by **six to eight degrees**, and killing all but the hardiest plants and trees.

With fewer plant species to feast on, many **plant-eating dinosaurs** began dying out, too. As did the **meat-eating predators** that dined on *them*.

The result? Within 30,000 years of that impact, **eighty per cent of all animal species** — and almost *all* of the **large reptiles** and **dinosaurs** — had **disappeared**.

Ouch. So it was an asteroid, then?

The asteroid or comet caused global havoc. And yes, it almost certainly **finished them off**. But had the *timing* not been *quite* so bad, the dinosaurs (or at least a lot more of them) might have survived it.

The TIMING? Why's that?

As it turns out, around **68–66 million years** ago, there were also massive **volcanic ash eruptions**, from volcanoes in central India. These eruptions went on for more than 30,000 years and may have dimmed the skies, altered the **climate**, and dropped global temperatures by **two to three degrees!**

It's hard to know which event came *first*, as dating such distant events that precisely is extremely difficult. But the chances are that the volcanic eruptions and climate change happened first — **weakening** many dinosaurs over thousands or millions of years.

Then when the deadly asteroid or comet *did* arrive, it brought a final end to the **Age of Reptiles**, and the **130 million-year reign** of the dinosaurs.

Boo. But SOME of them survived, right?

Many reptile species *did* survive, yes. Including **crocodiles**, **alligators**, **snakes**, **turtles**, **tuataras** and more. But of the dinosaurs, only the smaller, flying ones survived. The ones we know today as **birds**.

But why those, and not the others?

That's a very good question. Again, we don't know for sure. But as far as we can tell, it seems that small, **warm-blooded** species (like mammals and birds) and **large, cold-blooded** ones (like crocodiles) did OK. Or at least, they weren't entirely wiped out.

But **large, warm-blooded ones** (like pterosaurs and dinosaurs) didn't fare so well.

Wait, dinosaurs were warm-blooded?

Maybe not warm-blooded in the way that birds or mammals are. But they may have had slightly **higher metabolisms** than other reptiles — meaning that they could generate and retain body heat much more effectively.

Is that why birds survived, but other dinosaurs didn't? Because it was too cold for them?

That may have been part of it. But it may also be because the **non-avian** (non-birdy) dinosaurs **grew too slowly**, and had trouble competing with the **feathery**, **hairy** animals that replaced them.

I WISH I HAD A COAT!!

In any case, the disappearance of so many large predators left a lot of reptile-shaped gaps in the world. But it wasn't long before those gaps were filled . . .

Which predators ruled after all the dinosaurs died out?

After the death of most dinosaurs around 65 million years ago, the 'Age of Mammals' began. Before long, cats, dogs, bears and other hairy carnivores were topping food chains all over the planet. Plus, as we've already learned, not all

of the dinosaurs died out! Some went on to become fierce airborne predators, in the shape of owls, falcons, and other birds of prey!

Hang on! Why did birds and mammals win the fight?

How d'you mean?

I mean, why didn't the reptiles just rise up again?

You mean grow back into dinosaurs and reclaim the throne? For a second 'Age of Reptiles'?

Exactly!

Good question. It could be that the larger dinosaurs may have had more trouble adjusting to the cooler climate that immediately followed the asteroid strike. And compared with smaller reptiles, they may have had more trouble finding enough food to support their larger, more energy-hungry bodies.

Unlike **mammals**, large dinosaurs usually ate during the day and couldn't easily hide in the dark. Unlike **crocodiles**, they couldn't hide underwater. Unlike **birds**, they couldn't take to the skies to escape predators. And they may simply have grown too slowly, compared to their fast-growing competitors. In reality, it was probably a combination of these things that did the non-birdy dinosaurs in.

Did the dinosaurs really grow that slowly?

Compared to modern birds and mammals, yes.

In fact, lots of dinosaurs (especially the larger ones) grew **seasonally**, as trees do. Their bones show tree-like growth-rings, showing that they would grow for a while, then stop, then start growing again. Mammals and birds, on the other hand, grow more or less *continuously* from birth (or hatching) to adulthood.

So while the baby dinos still tottered around for months or years after hatching, similar-aged birds and mammals would already be fully grown, and *hunting*. Hunting for eggs and baby dinos . . .

So did most of the birds and mammals survive?

No, not at all. Most of *them* died out, too! In fact, of the two major groups of birds twittering about at the time, the more successful group died out almost immediately! The surviving family grew much faster, and later evolved into a huge and widespread class of birds, including predatory birds of prey like **owls**, **eagles** and **falcons**.

As for the **mammals**, not very many had evolved yet, as they were held in check by the dominant dinosaurs. But based on fossil finds from the period, it's fairly clear that soon after the asteroid exploded, the number of mammal species on the planet *exploded*, too.

So what kinds of animals were there?

That depends on how far back you go. The first mammals were **tiny**, **rodent-like** and **not too smart**. But within 40 million years of the demise of the (non-birdy) dinosaurs, there were huge, primitive **horses**, **rhinos** and **tapirs**; primitive **pigs** and **camels**; even **hippo**-like mammals that took to the oceans — eventually evolving into **whales** and **dolphins**.

Weren't there any predators around to scoff these things?

Of course there were. The largest (and most successful) predators to evolve during this time were called **creodonts**. These **hairy**, **toothy**, **meat-eating mammals** weren't quite cats, dogs or bears, but something in between.

Other mammals evolved into **miacids**. These were small, slender, meat-eating creatures that hunted in the trees, like modern **civets** and **pine martens**. Over millions of years, the miacids grew larger, smarter, and more ferocious — gradually evolving into **cats**, **dogs**, **badgers**, **bears** and other modern **carnivorous mammals**.

Some of these carnivores also took to the water, becoming aquatic predators like **otters**, **seals** and **sea lions**.

When did the first big cats and bears appear?

About **23 million years** ago. This was the time of *Thylacosmilus*, the marsupial sabre-toothed cat, which prowled South America in search of rodents and forest pigs, and of *Amphicyon* – the long-tailed, primitive bear with wolf-like teeth, which ruled North America until the true bears came along.

True cats (felids), dogs (canids) and bears (ursids) didn't arrive until just **2.5 million years** ago, along with **man-sized beavers** and immense **woolly rhinos** and **mammoths**.

Hunting these were the famous **sabre-toothed tiger** (*Smilodon*), the powerful **dire wolf** (*Canis dirus*), and the fearsome **giant cave bear** (*Arctodus*).

Wait a minute! When did the humans come along? Aren't we mammals, too?

We certainly are. The ancestors of today's monkeys and apes first appeared around **40 million years ago** and the first, ape-like **Hominins** around **15 million years ago**.

Our own particular mammal family, *Homo sapiens*, only arrived around **2.5 million years** ago.

WHAT DO YOU FANCY FOR DINNER?

Soooo . . . did any of those animals eat cavemen for dinner?

Many of these outsized mammal predators (like **cave bears** and **sabre-tooths**) died out at the peak of the Ice Age, unable to cope with the changing climate. Others — like **dire wolves**, **mammoths** and the long-extinct **American lion** —

were hunted to extinction by humans, or found themselves unable to compete with human hunters for prey.

The last **12,000 years** of history is known as the **Age of Humans**. During this time, we took up **farming**, built **civilizations**, and **spread out** to engulf every corner of the world.

This, not so coincidentally, also led to the gradual **extinction** of **most** other large predators on the planet.

Humans, it seems, don't tend to play so nicely with others.

That's awful.

This is why we need to learn more about other predators – including cats, dogs, bears, birds and others – so that we can find a way to live with them, and to protect them . . . which is what the *rest* of this book is all about!

Prehistoric Puzzler

Across

2 Name given to fossilized dinosaur poo (9)

5 Gliding 'dino-bird', whose name means 'ancient wings' (13)

7 Tyrannosaur found in China, whose name means 'Emperor Dragon' (6)*

8 Whale-sized, croc-snouted theropod that could have take T. rex in a straight scrap (11)

Down

1 Sail-backed reptile predator that ruled the Permian Era (10)*

3 Word meaning 'hunter' or 'thief', which comes after eo-, micro-, ovi- and veloci- (6)

4 Flapping, gliding, long-beaked reptile that first appeared in the Triassic Age (9)

6 Three-fingered forerunners of the Tyrannosaurs, which lived in the Jurassic period (10)

*You might need to look up this answer online as the dinosaur isn't included in the book.

70

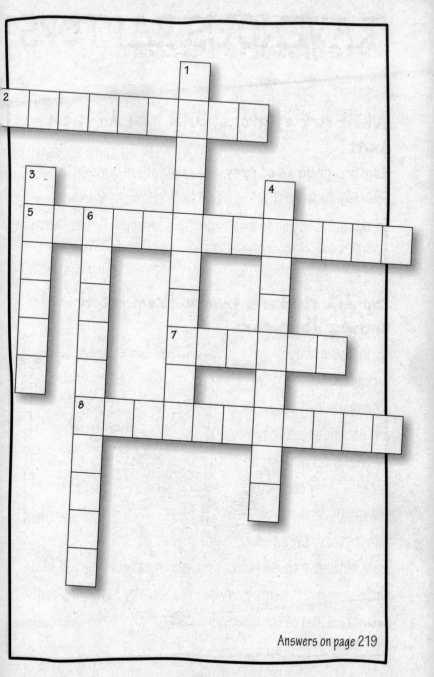

Answers on page 219

RAVENOUS RAPTORS

What are raptors, and how do they hunt?

Raptors, or **birds of prey**, are carnivorous birds with powerful beaks and talons. Like lions, tigers and other predators, they hunt meaty animals for food. But unlike other predators, they do it from the air.

So did raptors evolve from meat-eating dinosaurs?

Technically, they *are* meat-eating dinosaurs. But not all the dinosaurs they evolved from were meat-eaters. Many early birds ate snails, insects or fish instead. Even today, *most* birds eat these (and other, non-meaty) things. In fact, their varied diet is probably one reason why birds *survived* extinction and other dinosaurs *didn't*.

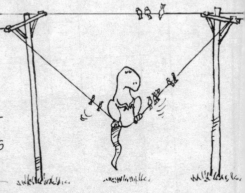

So what do raptors eat for dinner?

Generally speaking, raptors eat **other birds** or **mammals**. Raptors also have features and behaviours rarely seen in other birds. Things that give them more in common with predatory mammals like weasels, wolves and tigers.

Like what?

Generally speaking, raptors avoid snapping at food with their beaks, as other birds do. Instead, they hit their prey feet-first with their razor-sharp **talons**, and grip it until it stops struggling. Only then do they use their powerful beaks to shred meat off the bone.

Beak

Talons

Raptors also **stalk** and **ambush** their prey. Birds that eat snails, worms, or shellfish rarely need **tactics** like this, but rats, voles and rabbits are far more wary, scarper quickly when attacked, and are *much* harder to pin down.

To get around this, some raptors — like **Harris hawks** — hunt prey together in **teams** as wolves and lions do!

Pack-hunting hawks? That's pretty awesome.

Raptors also tend to **eat less often** than other birds. While seed, grain, and insect-eating birds have to find things to nibble all day, raptors get a lot more nutrition from each meaty kill. So between meals they spend much of their time snoozing and grooming — as dogs and cats do.

Where they differ from wolves and lions, of course, is that raptors spend the rest of their 'spare' time **flying**. This lets them cover **far more ground** than lions, wolves and other four-legged predators, and keeps them **safe** from ground-

based attacks. This may be yet *another* reason why raptors did so well compared to non-birdy dinosaurs.

So how many kinds of raptor are there?

More than you might imagine. Depending on how you group them together, there are at least **ten** families of raptors, with a wide range of different shapes, sizes and behaviours. In all, there are over **500** species of raptors in the world, covering every type of habitat from frozen **arctic** to the scorching **desert**.

Wow! I had no idea there were so many!

Just goes to show — in nature, the more adaptable you are, the better you fare . . .

Why do only little falcons hover?

All raptors can flap and glide, but not all of them can soar, and fewer still can hover. Flight can be a tricky thing, and though all raptors are masters of the air, their shape, size and weight all limit how they move through it.

So different birds fly in different ways?

Absolutely. All birds **take off** more or less the same way, but they **move through the air** in several different ways.

Take-off happens in one of two ways: **running and flapping**, or **dropping and gliding** from something high (like a cliff or tree). Scientists are still undecided about which of these birds did first.

Some say that small two-legged, feathery dinosaurs began jumping and flapping to catch airborne insects, or to escape attacks from ground-based predators. Others say flight began with claw-winged dino-birds that glided between trees.

Whatever the case, scientists agree that once a bird is **in the air**, in can keep itself there in one of five ways.

These are:
- **continuous flapping**
- **flapping and gliding**
- **bounding**
- **dynamic soaring**
- **thermal soaring**

What's the difference?

Continuous flapping is pretty much exactly what it sounds like. **Hovering** is a special type of continuous flapping, in which the bird stays in the same place as it flaps, neither gaining nor losing height.

All birds (except flightless ones like ostriches and penguins) **are capable of flapping**, but most don't do it for long. This is because beating your wings non-stop takes a huge amount of energy, and tires you out fast.

Even with wings strapped to their arms, humans can't do it hard enough to get airborne.

NOW YOU TELL ME!

This is where **gliding** comes in.

In **flapping and gliding**, the bird alternates between flapping its wings for speed and lift, and gliding forward with outstretched wings. This takes far less energy, and allows the bird to travel further without exhausting itself.

Bounding flight happens when a bird folds its wings between bursts of flapping — rising and dipping like a stone skipped across water.

Dynamic soaring is when a bird flying over open ocean uses updraughts of wind bouncing off the waves — keeping their long wings outstretched to catch as much wind as possible, and gliding upward and onward between updraughts, with very little flapping in between.

Thermal soaring is when a bird rides rising bubbles of warm air over land. These bubbles often form over fields, hillsides, buildings and roads,

which become warmer than the surrounding area during the day, creating **convection currents** in the air above as heat is transferred to and from the ground.

So why don't they all fly the same way?

Because raptors come in a range of shapes and sizes, and not all sizes and wing shapes allow for all types of flight.

Generally speaking, birds weighing over **five kilograms** are **too heavy** to stay aloft through continuous flapping. To get around this, they have evolved larger wings that enable extended **gliding and soaring**. Keeping these big, broad wings outstretched takes far less energy than flapping them up and down.

Why can't smaller birds soar, too?

Because air doesn't flow smoothly over tiny wings. Below a certain size, the drag created at a small bird's wingtips outweighs the lift provided by the rest of its outstretched wings. This is why you never see sparrows, swallows or hummingbirds gliding.

So basically, raptors fly the way they need to?

Exactly! They fly way they have *evolved* to fly – to fit their environment, to target their prey, and to get the job done. Of course, how they actually **capture** things is an entirely different story . . .

Why do vultures eat rotten bodies?

Because they **can**. Most predators do it from time to time. And it's a good thing they do. Without carrion-eaters, the world would be a far nastier place.

But eating corpses is GROSS! Why don't they hunt their own, fresh prey like lions and cheetahs do?

Think about it — even if you *could*, why would you *bother* competing with other predators like lions and cheetahs? Far easier to let them do their thing, then swoop in and steal a meal instead. True, the lions and cheetahs might not be too happy to see you. But that's a risk worth taking when you're hungry.

Also, depending on where you live, there might not *be* that many things around to chase. **Vultures** are **most** common in deserts and mountain regions.

In those places, prey can be hard to come by. So it pays not to be choosy about what you eat.

Don't they get sick?

Not often, no. Vultures actually prefer fresh meat if they can find it. But if not, they can easily survive eating meat so rancid with bacteria that it would kill lesser animals (humans included).

How?

In short, vultures' stomach acids are so powerful that they can burn you, and their digestive systems can absorb all but the chunkiest bone fragments. The powerful acids dissolve harmful bacteria and toxins before they can do any damage to the vulture. Humans simply cannot do this. But we should be happy that vultures can.

Happy? Why?

By eating all the dead, rotting bodies, vultures essentially hoover up the nasty, disease-causing bacteria inside them, and prevent them from reaching other animals. If eaten by people, or washed into wells and water sources, these bacteria cause gut diseases like **gastroenteritis**.

Worse yet, with no happy, corpse-munching vultures around, less efficient

scavengers like **rats** and **wild dogs** move in. These bring with them far worse diseases, such as **rabies**, **anthrax** and even **plague**!

Vultures save us from the plague?

In places where plague still exists, yep — they certainly do. This is why **protecting** vultures — perhaps not the *cuddliest* or *prettiest* creatures in the world — is so important. Of the **twenty-three** species of vultures worldwide, more than half are under threat. For the good of the planet, and ourselves, we need to protect and preserve these fascinating (and misunderstood) birds for future generations.

Besides, vultures are **awesome**. Turn over to find out why!

Top Ten Facts about Vultures

1 Unlike most raptors, vultures are very friendly, social birds, which often fly and feed together in groups.

2 Large vultures are masters of thermal soaring, and often wheel around in the same, rising air bubbles. This gives rise to the myth that vultures circle around dying people and animals, waiting to feed.

3 A flock of vultures wheeling around in the same thermal is called a kettle – as they look like steam rising from a boiling pot.

4 A flock of vultures dining on the same corpse is called a wake.

5 Condors may travel over 200 km (120 miles) per day in search of food. That's like flying from Dover to London and back, just for lunch.

6 Vultures tend to have blunted talons, as unlike other raptors, they don't need them for killing.

7 Vultures do not call or sing. They grunt and hiss instead.

8 Many vultures pee on their own legs after feeding. This helps kill the bacteria and parasites they pick up as they trudge over corpses.

9 When threatened by predators like lions and hyenas, some vultures will quickly vomit to drop weight, allowing them to take off faster.

10 The Bearded Vulture (or Lammergeier) cracks open tough bones by carrying them to great heights and dropping them on to rocks. They also do this to live tortoises.

According to legend, the famous Greek playwright Aeschylus was killed by a plummeting tortoise (or rather the Lammergeier that dropped it) in 456 BC. How's about that for an unhappy ending?

WHAT IS THAT WHISTLING?

Do eagles attack with their feet, or their beak?

All hunting raptors have sharp bills **and** sharp claws. But while raptors often use their bills to **finish off** their prey, they generally attack with their feet.

So all raptors have sharp beaks?

Yep. Pretty much *all* raptors have sharp bills made for **tearing** fresh (or old) meat from bone, and **shredding** it before eating. That said, different **families** of raptor have slightly different bill shapes.

Eagles and **vultures** have the thickest, most powerful bills – ideal for ripping large chunks from the bodies of large animals, alive or dead.

Smaller **hawks** and **falcons** have narrower bills with sharp ridges for breaking the backbones of their prey.

And a few smaller falcons, like the **snail kite**, have thin, hooked bills adapted for spearing snails, lizards and insects.

They all do that? Even little, fluffy owls?

Yep. *Especially* little, fluffy owls. As a matter of fact, owls are some of the deadliest, most terrifying hunters on the planet.

Yikes. So what happens to the ... err ... shredded mouse?

That depends on the type of raptor. **Eagles**, **vultures**, **hawks** and **falcons** either swallow the shreds whole, or store them in a little pouch in the throat, called a **crop**. The crop works like a little pre-stomach, storing food scoffed in a hurry for digestion – or feeding to chicks – later on.

BILL

THROAT

CROP

Owls, however, don't have a crop. So instead, they **swallow whole bits of animal** – like heads, wings, even entire bodies – **bones and all**. Later, they spew up the undigested bits as shiny, black **casts**, also known as **owl pellets**.

If you have a roosting box for owls in your back garden, this gives you an easy way to tell if there's anybody home. Owls are neat, tidy creatures that avoid spewing up in their own homes. So just look for piles of owl pellets on the ground outside the entrance!

Owls eat things ALIVE?!

Sometimes, yes. But usually, the prey will have long since snuffed it – having been **speared** or **suffocated** by the owl's no-less-terrifying claws.

All raptors have strong, muscular feet, with a strong, sharp claw or **talon** on each one. Most have four toes (and talons) on each foot – three pointing **forward** like fingers, and one pointing

backwards, like a thumb. Usually, the 'thumb' talon is the longest and sharpest.

Why's that?

Because talons are a raptor's main attack weapon. With these, raptors can **spear** through skin, **break** small bones, and suffocate prey in their deadly, crushing grip.

In a typical attack, the raptor will swoop or dive at its prey, hitting it feet first with all the speed it can muster. The impact alone can break the neck of a small mouse of vole.

But just in case, the raptor **grips** its prey hard with its front-facing 'finger' talons, then uses the 'thumb' talon to apply **crushing**, **suffocating pressure**, or to **pierce vital organs** and finish the poor animal off.

That sounds monstrous!

It is. And perhaps that's no coincidence. This attack method
is something eagles and owls share with their distant
relatives — claw-footed carnivorous **dinosaurs**
like *Velociraptor*.

How big do a raptor's talons get?

That depends on the raptor, and what it likes to hunt. Large
hawks need talons long enough to grab a vole or squirrel,
while the talons of an adult **harpy eagle** — which lives in the
forests of South America — are longer than the claws of an
adult grizzly bear. They're strong enough to crush a human

forearm, and sharp enough to pierce a human skull! Luckily for us, **harpy eagles** don't hunt humans – preferring **sloths**, **monkeys** and **boa constrictors**.

Phew! That IS fortunate.

Actually, as is so often the case, we are more of a threat to these fearsome predators than they are to us. Due to forest clearing in South America, the harpy eagle is now an **endangered species**. Yet another reason why we need to protect our predators (and their forest homes) for the future . . .

Focus: The Raptor Wrangler

Rebecca Krebs *is a former Assistant Curator of Birds at The American Eagle Foundation, and a Carnivore Keeper at Miami Zoo, Florida. There, she works with everything from sloth bears and hyenas to jaguars and giant river otters.* *Coolest. Job. Ever.*

Did you always want to work with animals?

Yes! I have loved animals since childhood. As a teenager, I raised farm animals, rode horses, cared for orphaned animals, and showed steers in fairs. Also, my father has had a zoo since I was a child. So I would spend my summers with him, caring for animals.

What is your favorite raptor, and why?

My favourite would have to be the
golden eagle. They are so very
intelligent. They can recognize
human facial features and tell
people apart from their voices.
They are so very strong and
powerful, but have the ability to
be soft and gentle. It has been an
honour to work with them.

What are the main threats to survival for endangered raptor species today?

Illegal shooting and habitat destruction are the two biggest threats to birds of
prey. Many people shoot birds of prey out of fear that they will kill poultry or
small pets. But mostly, that fear is based on myth and not fact.

What can we do to help ensure their survival right now, and for future generations?

Become educated and educate others on the importance of raptors in the
ecosystem. The better we understand them, the more likely we are to take
steps to ensure their survival. Big things we can do is get proactive in
preserving land for future generations. Too big a mission? Then do simple,
but big things, like recycle. Every little bit helps make a difference to all
creatures who share this planet.

What made you want to work with raptors?

It was an accident, really. I thought that it would be interesting to work with
them, so I applied as a volunteer with The American Eagle Foundation, and
promptly fell in love. They are fascinating creatures with unique personalities.
They are *so* much fun to work with. And I love to watch them fly.

What do 'hawk-eyed' and 'eagle-eyed' really mean?

All raptors have superb vision, and see up to **ten** times better than humans. No human pilot – no matter how 'eagle-eyed' – could ever hope to match them!

Does that mean they can see ten times further than us, or just ten times more clearly?

Probably *both*. Much of their success is down to their enormously powerful eyes. They can scan for targets at incredible distances, focus clearly at amazing speeds, and feed the raptor split-second information as it rips through the air towards its target.

So they're basically a huge, flying pair of eyes. With talons.

That's one way of putting it, yes. And that's probably how they look to a mouse or rabbit . . .

What makes their eyes so amazing?

Their *size*, for one thing. If you look at a human, our heads make up about **one-tenth** of our total body weight. Our eyeballs, in turn, are about **one-hundredth** the weight of our heads. In other words, should you so desire, you could cram about **fifty** pairs of human eyeballs into one empty human head.

Now let's look at a raptor. Hawk heads are about **one-tenth** the size and weight of their bodies, also. But their eyes weigh up to **one-fifth** as much as their heads! In other words, you could only cram **five** pairs of hawk eyeballs into one hawk head. So compared to their overall body size, hawk eyes are around **ten times** larger than human ones.

Is that all that's different?

Far from it. Hawk eyes, like human eyes, have a **pupil** (the hole through which light enters the eye), surrounded by a coloured **iris** (the ring of muscles that change the size of the pupil), a milky, white **sclera** (the 'whites of the eyes'), and a pair of protective **eyelids**.

Unlike human eyes — which sit **side-by-side** in a flat, human face — a raptor's eyes lie on **either side** of its long, narrow head.

*The exception to this are owls — which do have two, forward-facing eyes set side-by-side in their flattish faces. This gives owls better **binocular vision** — and **depth perception** — than other types of raptor. We'll learn more about owls in the next section.*

Does that mean they can't see straight ahead?

Not at all. Each eye can scan an area of about **150 degrees** to each side of the raptor's head, which allows the bird to scan a wide area to the side of (and even slightly behind) its own head for targets or threats.

But the visual field of each eye also **overlaps at the front**, giving the raptor **30–50 degrees** of double-eyed (**binocular**) vision. In short, they get all the benefits of wrap-around vision, plus all the benefits of forward-facing vision.

Plus — to protect their eyes — raptors have evolved something else we human don't have: flight goggles.

96

Goggles? Seriously? Why?

The same reason human car drivers and aeroplane pilots did — at least until windscreens were invented. No matter *how* good your eyes are, you won't be able to see very well with the wind rushing into them. At high speeds, the increased pressure of air hitting your eyes deforms the eyeball, preventing it from focusing properly, and bombards the delicate surface of the eye with dirt and grit.

Luckily, mutation, time and evolution have provided them with a second, transparent eyelid. These eyelids slip over the eyeballs during flight, protecting the eye from damage and keeping them focused, even at extremely high speeds.

Cooool. I wish I had natural goggles.

They would certainly make beach trips a lot more fun.

So what else do hawk eyes have that ours don't?

The rest of the magic lies **inside** the eye. Hawks, eagles and vultures all have super-flexible **lenses** inside their eyes, in turn connected to super-responsive **nerves** and **muscles**. These shift the **shape** of the lens in an instant, allowing the raptor to rapidly shift focus from **distant** objects (like a mouse on the distant but fast-approaching ground) to **close** objects (like the same mouse, half a second later!).

Like human eyeballs, hawk eyes contain a thin sheet of cells at the back of the eye called the **retina**. One particular section of the retina — called the **fovea** — contains more visual cells than any other part. This is the part that both humans and raptors use to focus on fine **details**, or pick out **tiny, distant objects**. Only raptors have *two* of these 'super-focus' spots, rather than one like we do. And theirs are many times more powerful than ours.

How much more?

Well, the fovea in a typical **human** eyeball contains around **200,000 visual cells** per square millimetre. But the fovea of an **eagle**, **buzzard** or **vulture** may contain up to 1,000,000 cells per square millimetre.

This, combined with the other features we've already talked about, gives eagles, buzzards and vultures **eight to ten times** better vision than humans.

Wow. What would that even look like?

It's pretty hard for us to imagine. But let's put it this way —
a **golden eagle** can spot a rabbit
hopping about on the ground
from over a mile away.

From **half a mile** (800
metres), it can tell how hard the rabbit is *breathing*.

And from a **quarter of a mile** (400
metres) away — the
length of **four**
Olympic swimming pools, or **eight**
full-sized football pitches — it can
see *every one* of the rabbit's tiny,
twitching whiskers.

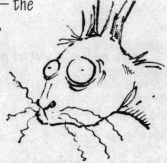

That is crazy! But if ALL raptors have awesome vision, why do hawks and eagles get all the credit?

Hmmm. Maybe because vulture-eyed isn't quite as catchy?

Are owls blind during the day?

That's a total myth. Owls see just as well as other raptors by day, and **better** than most raptors by night. The full list of owl 'superpowers' includes night vision, 3D hearing, and stealth flight — making them the terror of every tiny mammal!

Owls have SUPERPOWERS?

Totally. Most owls have super-powered senses that allow them to **see**, **hear** and **hunt** their prey in almost total darkness.

Can other raptors do that?

As we've already learned, *many* raptors have excellent eyesight. But only owls have acute **night vision**. And while a *few* other raptor species do have decent hearing, none have **three-dimensional hearing**, as many owls do.

Why not?

Because most raptors hunt by day, in plenty of light, they depend almost entirely on vision to locate their food. Owls, though, occupy a different niche. Though a few are out and about during the day, most owls are **nocturnal**. That means they sleep or hide by day, and **hunt by night**.

*Some raptors, including vultures, also have a keen sense of **smell**. But that, too, is rare in the raptor world.*

In fact, owls are the only truly **nocturnal** birds of prey. Because of this, they have evolved a variety of tactics and tools for hunting things that scamper in the darkness.

Weapons of 'Mouse' Destruction?

Very funny. But yes — something like that.

YEEEEAAAAHH!

The first secret weapon of the owl is, of course, their massive eyes. Owl eyes are **forward-facing** (like those of lions, tigers, and other mammalian predators), and are **extraordinarily large** relative to the size of their heads.

In low-light or near-darkness conditions, their huge, dark **pupils** open wide to funnel as much light as possible towards their super-sensitive **retinas**. This allows them to form a clear image where humans (and even other raptors) would struggle to make out more than a fuzzy outline.

If their eyes are so good, then why do owls always have to swivel their head round to look at things?

Because owl eyeballs are shaped differently to ours, and they can't move them about. **Human eyeballs** are round (or **spherical**) and have a circle of tiny **muscles** all around them. By activating these muscles, we can roll our eyes in their sockets to peek at things without having to turn our heads.

Owl eyeballs are more like **wide tubes** or **cylinders**. They point straight forward, funnel in plenty of light, and allow the owl to gauge the **distance** to a target very accurately. But tubes can't roll in their sockets. So if an owl wants to look at anything that's *not* dead ahead, it has to swivel its head and point its 'binoculars' somewhere else.

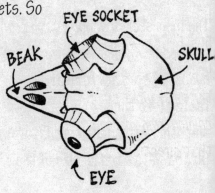

EYE SOCKET

BEAK

SKULL

EYE

To help with this, an owl's spine and neck muscles allow it to swivel its head through roughly **three-quarters** of a complete circle. Not quite *all* the way round, but good enough!

Creeeepy. What about when it's totally dark? What do they do then?

In *total* darkness, even an owl's eyes aren't much help. So the owl switches to secret weapon number two — 3D hearing.

Many mammals and birds can use their ears alone to tell the direction a sound is coming from. We call this **stereoscopic (or three-dimensional) hearing**.

It's done by comparing the time delay as the same soundwave hits first one ear, then the other. A sound coming from the left will hit the left ear *very slightly* before the right ear. So the brain picks up on this delay, concludes that *this sound is coming from your left*, and instinctively swivels your head in that direction.

Owl ears go one better. They're typically located just beside the eyes, one a little higher up than the other.

The ear-like tufts on the heads of some owls – like the long-eared owl – aren't actually ears at all. They're plumage for attracting mates. Something like a hip, spiky hairstyle.

This means they can not only locate which **side** of the head a sound is coming from, but also how **high up** (or **down**) the sound's point of origin is, relative to the owl's head. This 3D super-sense helps them pinpoint mice and voles in near-darkness.

Right before they swoop down and seize them from above.

Don't the mice see or hear them coming, and leg it?

Sometimes, yes. But in near-darkness, it's hard to spot an owl against a blackened sky or forest canopy. As for hearing their approach – well, that's where owls bust out secret weapon number three – **stealth flight**.

Generally speaking, owls hunt their prey using one of two tactics:

- Owls that hunt over open fields and plains like to glide low and slow like bomber planes, then swoop down to capture prey.

- Owls that hunt in dense woodland and forest prefer to fly from tree to tree, perch motionless above their prey, then drop on them from above.

In both cases, owls use their specially adapted feathers to close in on their prey, unseen and unheard. **Camouflage patterns** on their feathers hide owls as they perch and wait for prey. And **soft**, **downy flight feathers** decrease **air turbulence** at the edges and tips of their wings, making their flight almost completely silent.

So owls are masters of disguise, too?

Many are, yes.

Owls are basically feathery, airborne ninjas, right?

In short, yes.

Cooool. Makes me glad I'm not a vole, though.

Owl Search

At present, there are over 200 species known owl species throughout the world. Twelve are hidden in the grid below. How many can you find?

BARN

BAY

BOOBOOK

BURROWING

EAGLE

ELF

FISHING

GREATHORNED

SCOPS

SHORTEARED

SNOWY

TAWNY

```
B Z E A G L E Y L S M C V B C S V M Z V
S G B R K P E W M B A M J L N W B Q S A
R E S O N H L B Q R Z X N G S Y D C H B
E Z Y A O S W V P G K W R K Z C Q V O A
I Q M Y N B G Q T R E Y I V Z V P H R Y
C D M E J C O H E E P J C R P K Z S T O
H C X O G S Z O K A C P B S O N O N E K
Q I U F Q F X U K T H N W B N F T P A G
P R E R I Y C G H H V F R Q M V B C R E
T K B Y F J X D Q O X C V B C D P F E U
F J B D L G K F M R L J B L Z Y I D D M
B E U N D L E X C N B E V E N T B F P S
L C R U F N A X D E P A Y E Z X K E C N
H A R L F D V I N D S M R D J P L U I O
N A O B I T B C X W Q C I N K X E A E W
M M W K W L I N F I S H I N G T O I A Y
L N I K C L O Y T K M D E F Q F B O B L
V J N P B E S U M S J C U L J H J I O L
W R G I P G H K Z T A W N Y F W R A R K
B L S C O P S P A Y C A T E Q G N O I H
```

Answers on page 219

What preys on birds of prey?

Small raptors are hunted by many predators, including cats, dogs and other raptors. Larger raptors have few, if any, natural predators.

But all raptors can fly, right?

Right.

So how can other predators catch them?

Most raptors are very difficult to catch. But **cats**, **dogs**, **foxes** and other mammalian predators *can* pounce on raptors when they dive to catch prey,

perch on low-lying tree branches, or roost in rocky crevices close to the ground.

Most often, predators eat eggs or grab chicks straight from their nests. The same goes for egg-eating snakes. Some predators — namely other, larger raptors — may also hunt hawks and falcons in flight.

Raptors eat each other?

Sadly, yes. After all, raptors are carnivores, and if they're hungry enough ... well ... meat is meat.

For the most part, though, adult raptors don't have to look up (or over their shoulders) too often. They usually sit near the top of their local **food chain**. Only **humans** sit above them. But unfortunately, that can still be a major problem.

Why's that? Do we hunt hawks and eagles that much?

In some places, yes. Until quite recently, hunters in Europe, Australia and the USA used to stand on cliffs during hawk migration seasons, and shoot *hundreds* of them in a single day. These days, many raptors are protected by law.

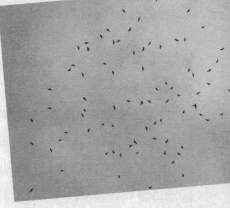

But they are still often shot by poachers and gamekeepers.

Why would anyone want to shoot a hawk?

For the same reason that people shoot **wolves**, **tigers** and other predators.

Some of this may be warranted. Hawks *do* hunt and kill ducks, pigeons and other game birds, and human gamekeepers and hunters don't take too kindly to raptors stealing their quarry.

But in other cases, the reasons make little sense at all. Farmers, for example, may shoot **hawks** and **eagles** to protect their sheep. Despite the fact that **raptors don't hunt livestock**.

Aside from this, most of the damage done by humans to raptors is indirect, or 'accidental'.

Wait – how do you kill something by accident?

Many hawks and falcons eat **rats** that have been **poisoned** by farmers. This poison often isn't enough to kill one rat. But it's more than enough to kill a raptor that eats *several* poisoned rats. **Road traffic** and **high-voltage power lines** kill *thousands* of raptors (along with other birds) every year.

But perhaps the largest threat to raptors is one shared by most of the world's predators – **habitat loss**.

So how does that work?

Raptors need **territory** in which to hunt. And plenty of it. As humans **clear forests** to create new **farmland** or **housing**, we destroy the natural hunting habitats that raptors have enjoyed for millions of years. Because of this, many raptor species worldwide are now under threat of extinction.

That's so sad. So what can we DO about all this?

Educate people! By talking to farmers, landowners and everyone else about the plight of endangered raptors – and giving them a chance to see the animals in another way – we can create a connection to these species and see them as important creatures, with real needs.

Birds of prey are often hard to see when in the air, so **zoos**, **sanctuaries**, and **falconry displays** can provide a special place for people to see the birds up close and see how majestic they truly are.

Know Your Stuff: Raptors Under Threat

Here are just a few of the raptor species that are currently under threat across the globe:

- The **Forest Owlet**, a tiny owl reduced by habitat loss to a tiny population in central India.

- **The Seychelles**, **Comoro**, **Anjouan**, and **Siau Scops Owls** – all threatened by habitat destruction in their forest island homes.

- The **Philippine Eagle**, driven close to extinction by timber cutting in its native rainforest home. Less than **500** now remain.

- The **Flores Hawk-Eagle** – a small eagle native to five small Indonesian islands. Thinned out by both forest cutting and poaching by farmers. Less than **150** now remain.

- The **Madagascar Fish-Eagle**, the largest native raptor in Madagascar, down to just **180** pairs after decades of forest cutting to clear space for rice paddies.

- The **California Condor** – the largest raptor in North America, poisoned by veterinary medicines fed to cattle, and eaten by the condor as carrion. Less then **100** now remain, all in captivity.

What is falconry (and can I do it)?

Falconry is the ancient sport of hunting with hawks, falcons and other birds of prey. In medieval times, falconry was practised by kings and nobles. Today, falconers can still be found throughout Europe, the Americas, and the Middle East.

So it's not, like, just keeping a pet falcon?

No. Birds of prey are *not* domestic animals. They are wild, predatory animals, and will *never* behave the way a pet cat, dog or parrot would.

Falconry isn't about keeping a plump, well-fed raptor in your house for fun. Frankly, raptors don't *like* people that much. What they *do* like is **chasing** and **catching** wild birds, rabbits, squirrels and other small mammals.

So falconry is more about providing **care** for a wild raptor, and **accompanying** it while it does what it does best: **hunting**.

Hmmm.

It's also a *lot* of hard work. First, you have to build a place to keep your raptor. This is known as a **mew** — a specially

designed 'raptor shed' with two or more perches inside. You also have to clean it out, practically every day, to stop the nasty build-up of blood, feathers, uneaten meat chunks and raptor poop on the floor.

Yuck! So what comes next?

Then you have to find yourself a raptor. In some countries, you're allowed to trap or net certain raptors from the wild. In others (like the UK), this is against the law, and you have to buy them from a licensed breeder. This may cost **hundreds**, even **thousands**, of pounds.

Once you have your raptor, you have to set about getting it used to working with people. This starts with giving it meaty treats on its own perch. Then feeding it perched on your gloved hand, or **gauntlet**.

Then enticing it to fly from perch to gauntlet. Eventually, after a lot more training, your raptor should be able to hunt outside over wide distances and still return to you.

Hang on – if the raptor is still so wild, what's to stop it from flying away once it's let out into the wild to hunt?

Absolutely *nothing*. Once loose, even after months or **years** of training, the raptor may still to fly off and hunt for itself, rather than return to the falconer for another snack. To discourage this, the falconer keeps careful track of the bird's weight.

How does that help?

Raptors are clever animals that will **stop** eating once they've had **enough**. The falconer, knowing this, weighs the raptor daily and figures out its ideal weight. Then he (or she) feeds the raptor just **enough** to keep it interested in coming back for more snacks, but never **so much** that it becomes full and refuses to hunt. It's a delicate balance.

Wow. So how did they figure all this out?

Falconers have had a *long* time to try, fail, think and experiment. There were falconers in ancient **Mongolian** and **Native American** tribes by 1000 BC, and there may have been falconers in ancient **Persia** (now Iran) as early as 8000 BC – more than 10,000 years ago!

So people are still doing it?

Absolutely. Today, there are still thousands of practising falconers worldwide. In **Asia** and **South America**, some falconers still hunt for a living as they have for thousands of years. Done properly, falconry can help to protect raptors and their natural habitat. But remember – caring for a wild raptor is no easy thing. So if you just want a pet, you'll be better off with a budgie!

Know Your Stuff: Royal Raptors

Today, most falconers stick to just a few species – like red-tailed hawks, Harris hawks, and kestrels (though some Mongolian tribes still hunt with golden eagles!). But in medieval Europe, a wide range of birds were used. The type of bird you kept usually suggested your status (or lack of it). These included:

Emperor – Golden Eagle or Vulture

King – Gyrfalcon

Earl – Peregrine Falcon

Knight – Saker Falcon

Lady – Merlin

Young man – Goshawk

Priest – Sparrowhawk

Servant – Kestrel

Focus: From Raptor Rescue to Falconry

April Davenport-Rice works with injured raptors at rescue centre in North Carolina, and hunts daily with her own red-tailed hawk. She is also President of the North Carolina Falconers Guild.

How did you get started working with raptors?

I'd always been an avid bird lover, but knew next to nothing about raptors. Then I got an opportunity to volunteer at the Carolina Raptor Centre, which takes in injured, orphaned or abandoned raptors, and it all started there.

So how did you become a falconer?

By accident! One day, two local falconers came into the Centre with an injured hawk they had found in a neighbour's chimney. I had no idea people even did falconry any more. Five years later, after learning all I could about how to care for the birds, I took the plunge, built my mews, and became an apprentice falconer.

What kind of bird do you hunt with?

Like most falconers here, I have a red-tailed hawk. My first one was a small male, which I released after my two-year apprenticeship ended. Now I have a larger female, and we've been together for three years.

How does falconry help to protect raptor species that are threatened in the wild?

In the USA, all raptors are protected by the Migratory Bird Act. But many are still under threat from habitat loss. Red-tailed hawks – the birds we work with most – have actually increased in number in recent years, because people throw trash out of their car windows. This brings rats and mice to the roadside, and the hawks just wait there to scoop them up. But sadly, this has also led to more impacts with cars, and more injured and orphaned raptors.

So how does hunting with birds help?

Falconers trap and train young birds that would otherwise not survive long in the wild. We treat injured feet and talons, and give them medicines to rid them of parasites that would have slowly killed them in the wild. Many falconers also buy and preserve acres of field and woodland, just for their birds to hunt. Falconry gives a reason for conserving raptor species and the habitats they live in. It has done so for thousands of years and, thankfully, is still doing so today.

CRAFTY CATS

What makes a cat a cat?

In short, stealth, whiskers and a taste for meat and fish! Cats come in all sizes — from 'big cats' like lions and tigers to the small, fluffy kitties in our homes.

Lions, tigers and pet kitty-cats seem pretty different to me! What do they all have in common?

Though cats vary in size, they *all* share very similar body shapes. In fact, when experts look at skeletons without the muscles and fur, even *they*

have trouble telling the difference between two big cats (like a **lion** and a **tiger**), or two small cats (like a **wildcat** and a **jungle cat**).

Like other predators, cats use their sharp **senses** to track and capture prey. Their rotating ears are sensitive to much fainter sounds (and much higher frequencies) than ours, and help them pinpoint the direction of a scuttling rodent or snuffling boar in near-darkness.

Their forward-facing **eyes** give them excellent **depth perception**, allowing them to judge the precise distance to their prey before pouncing. They also have a special **lens** that bounces light back towards the retina in low-light conditions, giving them **six times** better **night vision** than humans. (This also causes the freaky, laser-like 'eyeshine' seen in flash photographs.)

And in *total* darkness, their sensitive **whiskers** help them to feel their way past obstacles, and to sense changes in **air pressure** caused by prey moving nearby.

Wow. They're like fuzzy, hunting MACHINES.

Indeed. **Silent** ones, too. All cats are equipped for **stealth**. Their clawed fingertips (and toe-tips) fold back on themselves, allowing them to **retract their claws** to sneak up on their prey.

Once they get close enough to pounce, their powerful leg muscles come into play. All cats have extremely strong hind leg muscles, giving them explosive **pouncing** and **sprinting** abilities.

To top it all off, cat **teeth** are tailor-made for biting flesh. Their four large fangs (or **canines**) pierce and grip their prey during an attack, while the small, sharp **incisors** in between are used to tear meat from the body.

This done, sharp, cone-shaped **carnassial** teeth behind each cheek shear the meat into chunks before swallowing, and a rough **tongue**, covered in tiny **hooks** or **rasps**, strips feathers and fur from the prey's hide.

So THAT'S why my cat's tongue feels like sandpaper?

Yep. But don't worry — I'm *sure* she's not trying to eat you.

ROAR!

Which came first – big cats or little cats?

The first, prehistoric cats were small, tree-climbing creatures. But those went extinct over 20 million years ago. Big cats arrived a bit more recently.

20 million years? Wow – cats have been around for that long?

Yep. Cats are a hugely successful family of mammals. The earliest known cat-like animal, *Proailurus* (meaning 'first cat'), weighed just nine kilograms. It had a longish snout, lived in tree canopies, and looked more like a modern-day civet (more about them later). 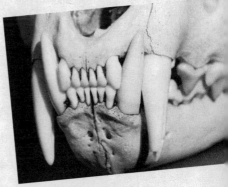 But it had all the major cat features — including **forward-facing eyes**, **carnassial teeth** and **retractable claws**.

Next came the ground-living *Pseudailurus* (meaning 'sort-of cat'), which came in a range of sizes from wildcat- to puma-sized. *Pseudailurus* first appeared around **20 million years** ago, and was probably the first cat to cross into the Americas, across the land-bridge that (back then) existed between Siberia and Alaska.

Nice! So what came after those?

Around **10 million years** ago, there was a split in the growing cat family. One branch evolved into fearsome **sabre-toothed** cats while the other branch evolved into smaller (but no less fearsome) cone-toothed cats.

Sabre-toothed cats were tiger-sized with fearsome, **28-centimetre-long** canine teeth. They prowled North America right up until the peak of the last Ice Age.

Yikes! Did they ever attack people?

Probably — as human hunters competed with them for prey. In any case, sabre-toothed cats were unable to adapt to the cooler Ice Age climate. They went extinct around 10,000 years ago.

So what happened to the other ones? The cone-toothed cats?

They evolved into all the marvellous cats, big and small, we still see around us today.

Of these, **cheetahs** and **pumas** (or something like them) evolved first. Palaeontologists have found fossils of these dating back almost **10 million years**.

After cheetahs and pumas came smaller, stockier **lynxes**. These hardy, hairy cats – and their smaller cousins, the **bobcats** – evolved around **six million years ago**. They soon spread throughout the Northern hemisphere, following **hares**, **foxes**, and **squirrels** deep into the snow-covered north.

Lynxes have **short**, **stubby tails**, **huge paws** and **long**, **dark tufts** of hair on their **ear-tips**. **Bobcats** have smaller bodies, smaller paws and less obvious ear-tufts.

What about lions and tigers?

Lions, **tigers** and other **big cats** belong to the **Panthera** family, which first appeared around **four million years** ago. So well *after* pumas, cheetahs and lynxes.

So what about the rest?

The other **thirty-six** cone-toothed cats include everything from **domestic** (pet) **cats** and **wildcats** to **ocelots** and **fishing cats**.

For a rough guide to the world's not-so-big cats, see opposite.

Know Your Stuff:
The Wide World of Felines

Here are some other claw-toting-pouncers you may have heard less about . . .

Serval – Long-limbed, huge-eared stalker of African grasslands. About twice the size of the average domestic moggy, the serval hunts birds and rodents, and has the highest hit rate (50 per cent) of any predatory cat.

Caracal – A little larger than a serval, this reddish-brown hunter of rats, hares and small antelope lives in the deserts and scrublands of Africa and the Middle East. Its long, tufted ears have earned it the nickname 'desert lynx'.

Pallas cat – Stocky, round-faced cat native to the Central Asia, about the size of a house cat, only much fluffier. Pallas cats have the thickest fur of any feline – their fuzzy coats and tails help keep them warm in the freezing winds of their habitat.

Jungle cat – Stocky, sand-coloured cats found throughout the Middle East and southern Asia. A little larger than the average domestic cat. A strong swimmer, the jungle cat hunts rats, reptiles, fish and frogs.

Sand cat – Tiny, blunt-clawed cat that digs for snakes and gerbils in the deserts of North Africa, where lions and leopards fear to tread. Also digs its own den, like a badger.

Clouded leopard – Small leopard relative native to China and Southeast Asia. An excellent climber, it stalks birds and monkeys among high tree branches.

Marbled cat – This elusive bird-hunter lives in the forests of Southeast Asia. It looks much like a tiny clouded leopard – the size of a house cat – and is so hard to find that scientists know little else about it.

Fishing cat – Semi-aquatic swimming cat that hunts fish, crabs and shellfish in the marshes, swamps and rivers of Southeast Asia. Who said cats don't like water?

Ocelot – Small, nocturnal cat that prowls the forests, swamps and grasslands of South America. This beagle-sized mini-jaguar eats everything from birds and bats to monkeys, turtles and armadillos.

Margay – Smaller cousin of the ocelot, which can reverse its back feet in order to run down trees like a squirrel. The least picky eater of all cats – dining on birds, mice, squirrels, possums, worms, spiders and even (occasionally) fruit.

Do big cats really eat people?

Despite their reputation, most big cats do their best to avoid people. When they do attack, it's often because they are sick, scared or desperate.

Aren't we, like . . . FOOD for big cats?

We *could* be. But we very rarely are. Big cats didn't evolve to eat humans. Their powerful bodies, sharp claws and keen senses all developed to help them hunt sturdy herbivores — like **boar**, **deer**, **horses** and **wildebeest**.

Big cats hunted these things for **hundreds of thousands of years** before humans came along. When we finally *did*, humans proved to be tricky, dangerous prey. With our nasty, hand-held **weapons** (first with clubs and spears, later with bows and rifles) and our tendency to **band together**, we simply aren't worth the risk.

So big cats aren't dangerous, then? I can keep a pet tiger, and cuddle it every day? Yay!

Whoaaaa, there. I didn't say big cats weren't *dangerous*. They can never really be 'tame' the way domestic cats are. And while they don't go out of their way to eat us, they can (and do) attack humans when they're **captured**, **cornered** or **denied their natural hunting space**.

But if lions and tigers don't often eat us, then where do they get their reputation as 'man-eaters'?

Well, lion, tiger and leopard attacks on people *do* happen.

The **Sundarbans** region between India and Bangladesh is home to about **600** Bengal tigers. Tigers there used to kill between 50 and 60 people per year.

In recent years, better land management and animal tracking has dropped the number of deaths to just two or three per year.

And in parts of Africa, lions and leopards (usually old, injured or diseased males) have been known to 'go rogue' and begin hunting isolated villagers and farmers.

But for the most part, unprovoked big-cat attacks on humans are not common. And much of their reputation as 'man-eaters' comes from the stories of hunters who blunder into *their* territory, competing for *their* prey.

Looked at this way, you can't really blame the cats.

I suppose not . . .

Before humans came along, big cats used to roam the entire globe. But now only five **Panthera** (or big cat) families remain.

These are:

lion (*Panthera leo*)
tiger (*Panthera tigris*)
leopard (*Panthera pardus*)
jaguar (*Panthera onca*)
snow leopard (*Panthera uncia*)

What about pumas and cheetahs? Aren't they big cats too?

Technically, no.

Why not?

Mostly because they cannot roar.

I DON'T WANT TO JOIN THAT STUPID CLUB ANYWAY!

Whaaaat?

All big cats have an extra-wide **larynx** (or voice box) and **hyoid bone** set very low in their **trachea** (or windpipe). This creates the deep, booming rumble we know as a roar.

Lions have the deepest (and loudest) roar of all, which they use to communicate. The roar of solo-living **tigers** and **leopards** is a little sharper and harsher, and they do it far less often. **Snow leopards** –

though they have all the necessary equipment – don't seem to roar at all. Which is still something of a mystery to scientists.

Maybe they don't want the mountain goats to spot their steamy breath in the cold air!

Could be. But if you're a goat, and you're close enough to see a snow leopard's breath, you've probably got other problems!

Why do tigers have stripes, but leopards have spots?

Stripes and spots help tigers, leopards, and other cats blend in with their natural environment. The choice between spots and stripes happened partly by chance – and partly due to the way the coat patterns are made.

Wait – tigers live in forests and jungles, right? And leopards live in forests or grasslands . . .

Right.

So how do orange-and-black stripes – or yellow and black spots – help them blend in with a green-and-brown forest?

Most can see at least one colour, so it's not quite black-and-white vision. But you get the idea.

Most of the animals hunted by tigers and leopards are **colourblind**. That means they can't tell the difference between green and orange. Spotting an orange tiger in the green jungle is much harder when you see everything in shades of grey.

135

Besides that, camouflage isn't about becoming totally *invisible*.

It isn't?

No. The best predators and prey animals can hope for is to become a little *harder* to see. Inspired by nature, human **armies** have been using camouflage for centuries.

Camouflage doesn't have to be **perfect** to do its job. It just has to be **good enough**. For tigers, leopards and other animals, this is fortunate — since no one *designed* their 'camo' patterns.

So how DID they get them?

They **evolved** them. At some point, the ancestors of tigers, leopards and other 'camo-cats' developed stripy or spotty coats. While not **perfectly** camouflaged, these stripy tigers (and spotty leopards) survived a little better than their plainer competitors.

Over thousands of years, the plain-coated tigers and leopards **died out**, while their better-camouflaged cousins **lived on**. And there you have it — **natural selection**.

But how do the patterns grow? Are tigers born with stripes?

Yes. Camouflage coat patterns develop in the **womb**, when the cat is still an unborn **embryo**.

Depending on the cat species, this camo-pattern can differ quite a bit.

- **Leopards** and have dark, ring-like spots (or **rosettes**) on their yellowish bodies, and dark spots on their tails
- **Snow leopards** have similar patterns, only on a whiter, fuzzier background
- **Jaguars** have similar markings to **leopards**, only with one or more small dots inside each ring
- **Ocelots** have elongated, **blob-like spots** on their bodies, and small, dark **spots** on their tails
- **Clouded leopards** have wide patches (with dark outlines on their bodies), and small, dark **spots** on their tails
- **Cheetahs** have small, **solid spots** on their bodies, which merge into **stripes** on their tails.

But only **one** species has a stripy body *and* a stripy tail — the **tiger**.

So why IS that?

Scientists used to think maybe it had something to do with where they live. In other words, **tigers** have **stripes** because they live in dense forest, while **leopards** and **cheetahs** have **spots** because they live among dry grasses.

The problem with that theory is that spotty **Asian leopards live in forests, too**. As do spotty **jaguars** and **ocelots** in South America.

So what's the answer?

We still don't know for sure. But many years ago, British mathematician **Alan Turing** suggested that animal camouflage patterns might be formed by **waves of chemicals** in the womb. If this were true, then one pattern of waves might give a **stripy** coat, while another might give a **spotty** one.

After years of research, it turns out he could be right. We still don't know what the pattern-making chemicals are. But using computer simulations, mathematical biologists have shown that **one** wave would lead to **stripy bodies and tails** (like a **tiger**), and that **two** waves would lead to **spotty bodies and tails** (like a **leopard**), or **spotty bodies and stripy tails** (like a **cheetah**).

If correct, this theory would also make it impossible to have an animal with a **stripy body and a spotty tail**. And as far as we know, no such animal exists!

WHAT?

So a leopard really CAN'T change his spots?

I suppose not. But then why would he want to?

Top Five Facts about Big Cat Camouflage

1 Tiger stripes are like fingerprints
No two tigers have the same stripe pattern. These stripes are especially varied on the face, making it easy for tigers to recognize friends and foes.

2 Snow leopards have the thickest coat of any cat
Their dense grey coats camouflage them against rocky cliff faces and insulate them against the freezing, high-altitude temperatures.

3 Black panthers are really just dark leopards or jaguars
A genetic mutation called **melanism** makes their fur dark, but not quite black. In direct sunlight, you can still see the spots and rings underneath.

4 White tigers are not a separate species
They're just normal (usually Bengal) tigers with a mutation called **leucism**. Being poorly camouflaged, white tigers do not survive long in the wild. So *all* of the world's white tigers are bred and kept in captivity.

5 Siberian tigers are not white, either
The rare Siberian (or **Amur**) tiger does survive (in very small numbers) in one, snow-covered area of eastern Russia. But like all other tiger subspecies, they are orange, not white.

Why do lions live in packs, but other cats stalk alone?

The grasslands of Africa can be a tricky place to hunt, and a dangerous place to live. For this reason, lions there live in packs to keep their cubs safe, and also to take on animals that would be dangerous to hunt alone.

Africa is a dangerous place for lions? Don't they basically rule the place?

In their natural environment, yes — *adult* lions are at the top of the African food chain. But lion *cubs* are not. Until they grow large enough to defend themselves, there is always the risk of an attack by another predator.

Like what?

African wild dogs, **jackals**, **hyenas** and **leopards**. These predators often attack when the mother leaves the cubs to hunt —

hiding them in long grass while she's gone. In fact, so many cubs are picked off by predators that usually less than half of each litter survives. Even then, the remaining cubs still may not be safe — as adult lions are known to attack cubs, too.

Lions eat each other?

Eat, no. But attack, yes. Male lions fight over territory and mates — sometimes to the death. And while a male lion will guard his *own* cubs from attack, he may attack those of others. When a male moves into a new group (or **pride**) and mates with a female, sadly, he may kill her existing cubs, to make sure that she cares for his — and only his — offspring.

This is one major reason why lions (or rather, lionesses) live together in prides. By forming a **crèche** with other mothers, sisters, aunties and nieces, lionesses can leave their cubs together to fend off attackers.

I always thought they grouped together for hunting and stuff.

Well, they do that, too. When lionesses go out to hunt, they often go together, in groups of three or more. If they're hunting something fairly small — like a warthog — a single lioness will sneak and pounce while the others just watch.

But if they're hunting larger prey — like zebra or wildebeest — then they may work together to separate a single animal from the herd while a single female closes in for the kill.

But tigers and leopards don't do that?

Tigers don't hunt large, herding animals on open plains or grasslands. They live in dense jungles and swamps. As for **leopards**, they do well enough hunting alone, and generally prefer to ambush prey by night.

As far as we know, lions are the only 'pack-cats' out there. So given that leopards live in the same place (and live alone), perhaps lion prides have more to do with defence than attack. Or perhaps lions just like hanging out with fur-friends!

Focus: The Mother of Lions

Mindy Stinner is the Executive Director and Co-founder of the Conservators Center, North Carolina. She oversees the rescue, upkeep and happiness of close to 100 animals – including lions, tigers, ocelots and binturongs.

Did you always want to work with animals?

I always wanted to work with animals, but at university I settled on Education and English teaching. Later, I began volunteering at a facility which housed many of the animal species we work with today. I knew my heart and soul was in working with these animals, and thought I should bring my education background to the problem. So we started our own facility.

Which cat species have you worked with?

Servals, caracals, ocelots, bobcats, jungle cats, Geoffroy's cats, lynxes, margays, mountain lions, and of course lions, leopards and tigers. I've also worked with a few even rarer species, such as fishing cats, jaguars, and snow leopards.

What is your favourite cat, and why?

I have a real soft spot for caracals. Of course, I was drawn to tigers first, because they're so charismatic. They're very individual and independent. They're not trying to fit in. If they want to go and jump in the pool, they'll do it. Afterwards, if they want to run, dripping wet, through a group of sleeping lions – even if they know the results may not be stupendously well-received – then they'll do that too. But I like the calm, serene, peaceful air of the caracal. And I admit to being utterly in love with lions.

What has surprised you about these animals?

Lions have their own little world, and see things a little differently to other cats. They're a very social cat. With them, you're held accountable for everything, and everything is a negotiation. I also did not expect lions to have a sense of humour. I can't tell you how many jokes the lions have played on us over the years.

Like, when they're babies, tapping you on one shoulder, and then standing behind the other. Or – when you offer them something – approaching you side-on to get it, and then knocking you over. They think that's the funniest thing. I expected all their play to be orientated towards hunting and killing. But they're also exercising their brains, figuring things out. To them, getting away with practical jokes and pranks is . . . well . . . hilarious.

Why do cats get stuck in trees?

Thanks to their claws and body shapes, most cats are really good at climbing up. But for the same reason, most have trouble climbing straight down. That said, some 'tree cats' are quite at home among the branches.

So cats are great at climbing up, but rubbish at climbing down?

For the most part, yes.

Why's that?

It's mostly down to **paws** and **claws**. All cats have handy, hooked claws which (in theory) should make them ideal climbers. It's as if they're walking around with built-in climbing axes and crampons. But just like these metal hooks and shoe-spikes, a cat's claws can only grip in one direction.

When a cat climbs up a tree, it does so with all four paws pointing straight up. The tips of its claws point downward, hooking into tree bark and supporting its weight against the pull of gravity.

Not *all* cats can do this, of course. Some big cats — like **lions** and **tigers** — are just too heavy. The largest tree-climbing cat is the **leopard** — which is about half the weight of a lion or tiger.

So why can't they just climb down again the same way?

Because their 'grappling hooks' don't work when they point the other way. Think about it — if a cat heads down a tree, nose first, its paws point towards the ground, but its claws point **upwards**. Angled this way, the hooks offer no support against gravity, and the cat is sliding face-first towards the ground.

Monkeys, apes and humans get around this by descending feet first. Below a certain height, cats will try this, too — hugging the trunk and slipping precariously downward for a few feet, then leaping to the ground when they get low enough. But they're not really built for this method, and they know it.

In the wild, cats **avoid** climbing higher than they know they can descend, and thus avoid the problem. But domestic cats

are sometimes too daft to know their limits. So they sit, terrified, in treetops for hours on end. Some may jump or climb down when they get hungry enough. Others have to be rescued by the fire brigade.

Silly kitties . . .

Indeed. But not all cats are so helpless in trees. In fact, some are quite at home there.

In the forests of South America, tiny, agile **Geoffroy's cats** leap and rebound off tree trunks like *parkour* experts, so get around the 'climb down' problem with descending jumps.

Margays, also native to South America, go one better. Their back feet rotate 180 degrees to face their tails, allowing them to run straight down tree-trunks, nose-first, or even to dangle from a branch by one back paw!

Know Your Predators: Geoffroy's Cat

Geoffroy's Cats hunt the forests and scrublands of South America. They are solitary creatures that bound and scamper between trees, hunting **frogs**, **birds** and **lizards**.

Geoffroy's cats are **crepuscular**, meaning that they are most active around dawn and dusk, and typically have spotted, camouflaged coats. They are also good swimmers, plunging into water to catch fish, and when necessary, crossing fast-flowing rivers over 30 metres wide.

At just **3–5 kilograms** when fully grown, they are smaller than most domestic cats. Which just goes to show – the best things often do come in small packages!

Tree kitties! Never heard of those. Are they the only ones?

A few other rainforest cats, like the **marbled cat** and **kodkod**, hunt in trees, too. But they split their time with hunting on the ground, and aren't *quite* as skilled as margays. Some of their cat-like cousins, though, spend almost all their time in treetops.

The wider family of cat-like mammals (or **Feliformes**) includes not just cats, but also **genets**, **civets**, **linsangs**, **binturongs** and other tree-climbing predators you've probably never heard of!

Wow! What are they like?

Genets are pointy-nosed, cat-like creatures with retractable claws that live in central and southern Africa. They're nocturnal — hunting rodents, wild birds and eggs by night. Perhaps the coolest thing about genets is that they're known to **ride on the backs of rhinoceroses**.

Possibly to avoid being eaten by leopards and hyenas. But possibly because it's great fun.

Civets, **palm civets** and **linsangs** are similar cat-like mammals that live in the forests of Southeast Asia. **Civets** are small, spotty-coated animals that hunt rodents and insects. They're good climbers, but spend much of their time hunting the forest floor.

Palm civets spend more time in trees, eat figs and other fruit, and sometimes get tipsy on fermented palm juice! **Linsangs** are gorgeous, slender, civet-like creatures that hunt frogs, snakes and rats in the jungles of Thailand, Laos and Myanmar – 'swimming' effortlessly between branches as they go.

Cooooooool!

There's more. Civets and genets are in a family of cat-like mammals called the **Viverrids**. The largest of these is the **bearcat** or **binturong**. Binturongs also live in the jungles of Southeast Asia, but grow up to *two metres* long – including almost a metre of long,

furry, muscular tail. These strange, slow-moving predators hunt birds, insects and small mammals, but also eat plant shoots and fruits when they can find them.

Baby binturongs up to three months of age smell like popcorn, but when attacked, can shoot a foul-smelling, sticky goo from a gland beneath their tails – much as North American **skunks** do. After three or four months, this goo-gland dries up, and they defend themselves with sharp claws and teeth instead.

Tree-cats, bearcats, and rhino-riding chicken hunters? These just became my favourite predators, EVER.

Time to book a jungle holiday!

Why don't cats dig holes or chew bones?

Cats like to keep their claws nice and sharp, so most avoid digging because it blunts them. But there are a few 'burrowing cats' in the larger feline family. And some like to gnaw bones, too . . .

Wait – there are burrowing and scavenging cats, too?

Yep. While they're not exactly *cats*, **meerkats**, **mongooses**, **aardwolves** and **hyenas** are all in the larger grouping of cat-like predators called **Feliformes**.

What? Meerkats and hyenas, too? Just how big is this kitty clan?

Huge. Aside from the **41** species of **Felids** (true cats, like lions, tigers and ocelots), this cat-like clan also includes:

- **33** species of **civet** (**Viverridae** – the forest-dwelling 'tree cats' we met in the previous section)
- **34** species of **mongoose** and **meerkat** (**Herpestidae** – 'burrowing cats' or 'creeping cats')

- **4** species of **aardwolf** and **hyena** (**Hyaenidae**, or 'pig cats')

Burrowing cats and pig cats?

It's true! Of these, **meerkats** and **mongooses** and perhaps the most enthusiastic burrowers.

Meerkats are small, weasel-sized predators that hunt lizards, insects and small mammals in the deserts and scrublands of southern Africa. There, they dig large, maze-like burrows and live in colonies of 30 or more.

Meerkats hunt by day, and while the rest of the pack forages for food, keen-eyed sentries stand up on their hind legs to keep a lookout. When they spot snakes, hawks or other predators, they chirp warnings that tell the others to watch out.

Amazingly, they have different warning sounds for ground-based dangers (like snakes and foxes) versus airborne ones (like hawks).

Mongooses (or mongeese!) live throughout southern Europe, Asia and Africa.

Yellow mongooses hunt birds, eggs and insects in southern Africa, and live in small family groups inside burrows, much like those of meerkats.

Dwarf mongooses, also native to Africa, burrow into termite mounds and stay there for days on end, solving their food and housing problems all at once!

Grey mongooses live in the forests of India, Nepal and Pakistan, where they hunt rats, scorpions and venomous snakes. These bad-boys have thick skins to protect against bites and stings, and are almost immune to cobra venom. **Crab-eating mongooses** live throughout Southeast Asia, burrowing for grubs and insects in the forest floor, but also plunging into rivers to catch fish, frogs and (you guessed it) fresh, tasty crabs.

But they're not the only cat cousins that like to dig. **Aardwolves** and **hyenas** do it, too. Aardwolves burrow for termites and grubs. And both aardwolves and hyenas dig dens to protect their young.

Wait a minute – hyenas and aardwolves aren't cats. They're dogs, aren't they?

Well technically they're neither cats *nor* dogs. They're in their own family entirely. But just as dolphins are closer to cows than sharks, hyenas are closer to **cats** than **dogs**.

But how can we tell? I mean, they look more like dogs, don't they?

True, in many ways, they do. They have longer snouts than most cats, forming a dog-like muzzle. They have broader bodies, and walk on flat feet rather than tiptoe.

But look *inside* a hyena or aardwolf and you see signs of their kitty-clan membership. They have fewer teeth than dogs, and fewer bones around their inner ear. And when you look at their DNA, you see that they're much closer to cats and civets than they are to the wild dogs and jackals that share their African home.

Like sharks and dolphins, **hyenas** and **jackals** are examples of what biologists call **convergent evolution**. This is when two animals *look* related because they've adapted to fit similar environments. But surprisingly, they're hardly related to each other at all.

But they still chew bones, right?

True. In fact, hyenas have the strongest bite of any animal their size. They even eat parts that lions and leopards leave behind, like hair, hoofs and horns. What they can't digest, they spew back up — much as owls do with their bone pellets.

Anything that chews bones is a dog in my book.

OK … but lions chew bones, too, you know? As do tigers, jaguars, giraffes …

Fine – you win!

Top Five Facts about Spotted Hyenas

1 They live in clans
Just as lion groups are called prides, hyena packs are called clans. A single clan may contain up to 50 hyenas.

2 The girls are the bosses
Hyena clans are led by females. The 'alpha' female is called the matriarch. Male hyenas rank below all females.

3 Females are larger and more aggressive than males
The average female hyena weighs around 80 kilograms, which is 20 kilograms heavier than the average male.

4 They eat fast
A small group of hyenas can go through an entire zebra in a little under 30 minutes. That's like eating 2,500 quarter-pounder hamburgers. Only with bones.

5 They don't really laugh
The famous high-pitched giggle of the hyena isn't a laugh at all. It's just one of many vocalizations they use to communicate fear, agitation or nervousness.

Is there an animal that hunts tigers?

Yes, there is. *Us*. Before humans came along, tigers, leopards, lions and other big cats covered most of the globe and had

no natural predators. But after thousands of years of competition, hunting and habitat destruction, many big cat species have disappeared from the world forever, and others are frighteningly close to doing the same.

There used to be big cats EVERYWHERE? Like lions in Europe, and cheetahs in America?

Yep. Pretty much. With the exception of Australia and Antarctica, big-cat territories used to span the entire globe.

Why none in Antarctica or Australia?

Antarctica was too cold and remote to support large, land-based predators like lions and tigers. With temperatures dropping to −90°C and nothing but tiny, agile penguins to prey on, it's not an easy place to hunt (notice there are no bears there, either).

As for **Australia**, it *did* once boast **marsupial lions** *and* **Tasmanian tigers**. But these were not actually lions, tigers or even *cats*. They were carnivorous **marsupials** – long-snouted, pouched mammals more closely related to the kangaroos and wallabies they hunted.

So what happened to them?

Sadly, all but **five** big cat species have **disappeared entirely** from the Earth. Some died out during the last Ice Age, but others – like the **cape lion**, **barbary lion**, **Caspian tiger** and **Javan tiger** – were driven to extinction by humans within the last 100 years.

The last known photo of a Javan tiger, 1938.

That's so sad. Couldn't we just stop hunting big cats now, and solve the problem?

Sadly, human hunters are not the only problem for big cats.

We've certainly hunted our fair share of lions and tigers. Since the invention of **firearms**, *thousands* of **lions**, **leopards** and **tigers** have been killed 'just for fun' by **trophy hunters**. Thousands *more* have been killed for their **pelts**, or for **teeth** and **bones** used in traditional Asian **medicine**.

But of all the things we do to harm big cats, **habitat destruction** is by far the biggest threat to their survival. It's not that we're *trying* to wipe them out. We humans just aren't very good at *sharing*. And this rarely works out well for other animals.

How's that?

Put simply, we humans are very good at moving into new territories and **owning** them. We clear forests, plant crops, capture livestock, build houses, villages, towns, cities, factories . . .

In the process of building these huge, **human-friendly playgrounds**, we tend to push other species out. Some species adapt well to human habitats. Others — like **big cats** and other large predators — not so much.

It's happening everywhere?

Yep. *Everywhere.* In **West Africa**, lions have been forced into smaller and smaller territories, as their natural homelands have been swamped by growing villages, towns and cities. In **South Africa**, lions survive on huge land reservations, protected by law. But who knows how long it will be before farms and villages start to appear inside these, too.

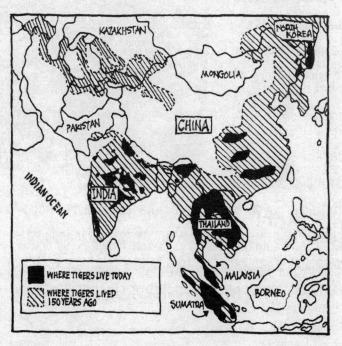

In **Southeast Asia**, **tigers**, **leopards** and **snow leopards** have been steadily losing their habitat to humans, too. Few tigers or leopards remain *anywhere* in **China**, **Vietnam** or **Indonesia**, and where tigers once roamed *throughout* **India**, they now survive only in small pockets.

Even **snow leopards**, hidden high in the remote mountain ranges of the **Himalayas**, have lost over 80 per cent of their natural habitat to livestock farmers. Less than **5,000** of them remain. Which may seem a lot, but really isn't.

So how can we save them?

First, we have to stop causing the problem, by being careful about how we live, what we buy, and what we eat. Obviously, buying tiger-skin rugs and leopard-skin coats is bad for big cats in the

wild. But so is buying **beef**, **soybeans**, **cotton**, **rubber** and **palm oil** from farms in Brazil, West Africa and Indonesia — from farms built on top of cleared rainforest, smack-bang in the middle of natural **jaguar**, **ocelot** or **tiger** habitats.

If we buy foods from local farmers instead, and look carefully at where our clothes and other goods come from, we can stop **supporting** the growth of farms like this, and help stop the habitat destruction they cause.

You could also join a local conservation group, volunteer to work on conservation projects, or raise money for others doing the same. Groups like this are already working with governments across Africa, Asia and South America to **educate** people about endangered species, **protect** forest and other cat habitats, and find ways to **help people and predators coexist**.

You mean live side-by-side in the wild?

Exactly. After all, **other** animals have managed to do this for millions of years. So maybe there's hope for us humans, too . . .

Feline Fancier's Crossword

Know your genets from your Geoffroy's cats? Then try this tricky, feline-inspired puzzle.

Across

3 Another name for the Asian bearcat (9)

4 Name given to a group of hyenas (4)

6 Group-living African predator that chirps a warning when it sees a snake or hawk (7)

7 The only big cat native to South America (6)

8 Pointy-nosed, cat-like mammal that rides on the backs of rhinos (5)

9 Stocky cat with huge paws and tufted ears, common in Canada and Russia (4)

Down

1 Slender, snake-eating feliform which is immune to bee stings and cobra venom (8)

2 The rarest of all big cats (4, 7)

5 Name given to a group of lions (5)

6 Tree-climbing cat that can reverse its back fee (6)

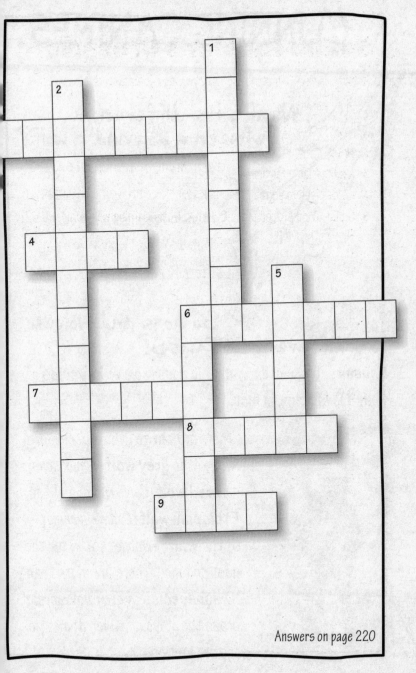

Answers on page 220

CUNNING CANINES

What's the difference between a dog and a wolf?

Dogs come in a range of shapes and sizes, and some of them may look somewhat wolfish. But dogs and wolves are quite different animals.

So dogs and wolves are different SPECIES?

Not quite. Technically, domestic dogs are a **subspecies** of wolf. One of many, in fact.

There are **three** living species of wolf – the **grey wolf** (*Canis lupus*), the **red wolf** (*Canis rufus*) and the **Ethiopian wolf** (*Canis simensis*). Of these, grey wolves are by far the most common. There are more than **20 subspecies** of grey wolf spread across the globe, of which domestic dogs are just one.

Wait, so you're telling me all dogs – everything from a dachshund to a Doberman – they're all just one, tame type of wolf?

Basically, yes.

That can't be right? I mean, those dogs look more different to each other than wolves do to . . . I dunno . . . huskies or German shepherds.

That's because we've been breeding dogs for thousands of years to generate different shapes and features.

But underneath, they're *all* the same animal — *Canis lupus familiaris*. The humble, domestic dog.

If dogs can look that different and still be the same species, how do you tell a wolf from a dog?

If you look closely enough at their bodies and behaviour, it *can* be done.

Starting at the **head**:
Wolves have smaller, thicker, and more rounded **ears** than German shepherds and other wolf-like dogs.

Wolf **eyes** are slanted, almond-shaped, and are rimmed with a dark, heavy outline (almost as if they're wearing eyeliner), and are *never* pale blue, like those of huskies.

A wolf's bone-crushing **teeth** tend to be larger and more curved than those of similar-sized dogs.

Moving to the **body**:
Grey wolves have narrower **shoulders** and **hips** than large dogs, and a layer of thick, wiry hair — called a **dorsal cape** — which starts at the back of the neck, falls over the shoulders, and runs right down the spine.

Wolves are slightly bow-legged in the back legs, and their front feet splay outwards when they sit.

Wolf **paws** are larger than those of similar-sized dogs, and their middle toes stick out, making them seem longer.

Wolves also have **webbed skin** between their toes (probably to increase their surface area for snowshoeing), while dogs do not.

Dogs and dog-wolf hybrids are often born with pink **pads** on their feet, which darken as they age. Wolf cubs *never* have pink pads.

Dogs have **sweat glands** in their paws, while wolves **do not**. And perhaps most obvious of all, many dogs have **white**, **pale**, or **pinkish nails**, while adult wolf claws are always **brown**, **dark grey** or **black**.

There are a few obvious differences in **behaviour**, too. When wolves **walk**, they place their back feet inside the footprints made by their front feet, creating **single-track footprints**. Dogs do not.

SSHHHH!

Wolves vocalize (or talk) using many different sounds — ranging from high-pitched yips and screams to lower puffs, growls and howls. But they **do not bark**, as domestic dogs do.

And of course, wolves tend to **avoid people** wherever possible, while dogs tend to seek them out.

So if wolves avoid people, then where did the first dogs come from?

Scientists reckon the first wolves were domesticated by European hunter-gatherers somewhere between **20,000** and **30,000 years ago**. But it's highly unlikely that they did it by snatching and training wild, adult wolves.

Some scientists think the hunters kept **orphaned wolf pups** after killing their adult parents, and tamed them that way.

Others think that the **wolves adopted us** — the braver, less cautious wolves venturing close to human settlements to steal food, being fed by villagers, and eventually kept around as handy guards.

So which was it?

We may never know for sure. But in any case, thousands of years on, 'man's best friend' is definitely here to stay. There are now at least **400 million** dogs kept as pets worldwide. That's about half the population of **Europe**, or more **dogs** than there are **people** in the *whole* of the USA!

That's one, big pooch party!

Are wolf packs dangerous to people?

Wolves, jackals and coyotes all pack together to hunt. But humans aren't on their list of normal prey. Unprovoked attacks on people by healthy wolves are rare, and attacks by jackals and coyotes, even rarer.

Do all wolves and doggy things live in packs, then?

Not all of them, no. Of the nine living families of dog-like carnivores, eight contain animals that live mostly alone or in pairs. These include **bears**, **raccoons**, **skunks**, **otters**, **weasels**, **wolverines**, **seals** and **sea lions**.

Only one dog-like family forms packs more often than not — the **canid** family. The canids first evolved around **30 million years ago**, and split off from bears, raccoons and other dog-like animals a few million years later.

Around **10 million years ago**, the family had evolved into two smaller tribes: the **vulpines** (**foxes**), and the **canines** (**jackals**, **wolves**, **dogs** and **coyotes**).

Prehistoric dog tribes? Cool! So which came first?

The oldest common ancestor of all the canids probably looked more like a fox than a dog or wolf. So I guess you could say that the foxes came first. Next came the **jackal**, the **dhole** and the slender, long-nosed **Ethiopian wolf** (which looks so much like a jackal that many scientists believe we should call it the Ethiopian jackal instead).

A little after that, within the last **2 million years**, came the **grey wolf**, the **singing dog**, the **dingo**, the **red wolf**, the **coyote** and (most recently of all) the **domestic dog**.

I've never heard of half of those. What's a dhole when it's at home? And a singing dog?

Jackals are tawny-coated, foxy-looking canines that prey on everything from birds and rodents to small sheep and cattle. Jackals tend to hunt alone, or in pairs, but may form small packs around breeding seasons.

Coyotes are the jackal's American cousins. Roughly one-third the size of grey wolf, their prey includes fish, rodents, sheep and deer. Though they generally hunt alone, they may form pairs or small packs to hunt larger prey.

Dholes (also called **Asiatic wild dogs** or **Asian red dogs**) are rare, red-coated canines found in parts of India, China and Southeast Asia. Dholes form small packs and hunt pigs, goats and small livestock.

So these wolf, jackal and coyote packs – do they ... y'know ... hunt people?

In spite of their reputation – no, they don't. Jackal and coyote attacks on humans *do* occasionally happen. But when they do, it's almost always a lone animal infected with **rabies**.

What Is Rabies?

Rabies is a nasty viral disease that infects wild mammals (particularly canids), causing brain inflammation, aggressive behaviour, and eventually, death. Humans can catch it, too, from being bitten by an infected animal.

What about wolves?

In almost all parts of the world, attacks on humans by wolves are very rare. When they *do* happen, it's almost always a lone, rabid wolf that attacks, rather than a ravenous pack.

On balance, we pose a far greater threat to wolves than they do to us. Left in peace, with their own territory and prey, wolves will happily avoid all human contact. And they certainly don't roam the wild, looking for hikers and backpackers, any more than they hunt little pigs or girls in red, hooded overcoats.

I guess the big, bad wolf isn't so bad after all!

Focus: The Wolf Whisperers

Kim and Frank Pyne *are working volunteers at the Conservators Center,*
North Carolina. Together, they researched and designed the entire upkeep
program for the centre's Alaskan grey wolves. In doing so, they formed an
extraordinary bond with the pack . . .

How did you end up part of a wolf pack?

When we came to the Center we began
work with Amadeus and Hopa – their
existing pair of wolves. When the new
cubs arrived, we helped raise them.
We began bottle-feeding Trekkie and
Roland when they were three weeks old,
and have spent over a thousand hours
with them.

What made you want to work with wolves, specifically?

Early on, our imaginations were captured by stories of wolves we heard growing
up. As we got older, stories gave way to science, but these complex, social

predators were no less amazing. So given the chance to work *hands-on* with wolves, we jumped at it.

In learning about these animals, what has really surprised you?
One fascinating thing about them is the depth and subtlety with which they communicate. From facial expression to posture, vocalizations . . . even subtle changes in scent that humans can't detect.

What are the main threats to survival for wolves in the wild today?
In a word, humans. The delisting of wolves from the Endangered Species List has allowed the wide-scale hunting of wolves – which not only kills individual animals, but also disrupts the social structure of packs.

How do you feel about re-wilding and other efforts to bring wolves back to their former habitats?
Having wolves returning to the wilds where once they roamed certainly *sounds* amazing. But in reality, it's a complex and difficult thing to do. We need to show people the benefits of their presence in the wild, and how to successfully live with them. That's why we do what we do.

What makes foxes so sly?

Foxes are the world's most successful dog-like predators. They are found in almost every corner of the planet, and tales of cunning, mischievous foxes are told from Africa to Australia.

So foxes live everywhere?

Fox species are found on *every* continent in the world, except Antarctica.

The **red fox**, the most common species, is found throughout the Northern hemisphere, from **Alaska** to **Siberia** and **Southeast Asia**, and also in **Australia** (brought there by British hunters in the early nineteenth century).

Their reddish fur, bushy tail, and white underbelly make them instantly recognizable and distinct from other canines.

Further north, white or blue-grey **Arctic foxes** inhabit the icy, snow-covered landscapes of the Arctic tundra, right across northern Canada, Scandinavia and Russia.

Further south, **kit foxes**, **fennec foxes**, **corsac foxes** and **Tibetan sand foxes** hunt the dry deserts of the Americas, North Africa, and central Asia.

By sleeping underground and venting heat through its huge, bat-like ears, the tiny **fennec fox** can survive the middle of the Sahara desert — in temperatures that swing up to **46°C** by day, and down to **4°C** by night.

So what makes them the top dogs?

Like all canine predators, they're **omnivorous**. In

182

addition to birds, rodents, rabbits and other small mammals, foxes will happily munch away on insects, grasses and flowering plants. And they're certainly not above stealing, scavenging, or eating carrion (dead things).

That said, foxes are *formidable* predators. Unlike cats, foxes and other canines have fairly poor eyesight. But their **ears** are nothing short of incredible.

Foxes can hear high-pitched sounds up to 65,000Hz, at a range of up to 160 feet — ideal for finding rodents scuttling through leaf litter or snow.

Their preferred method of attack is to pinpoint their prey through sound, then leap high into the air, coming down feet first, and pinning their prey to the ground for the lethal bite. Amazingly, this 'fox pounce' finds its mark more than 70 per cent of the time! Scientists aren't sure

how, exactly, they do it. But some think they may have an inbuilt, magnetic 'compass sense' that helps them track targets. This may also explain the fox's uncanny ability to elude capture, and their reputation for trickery and cunning.

If foxes are so smart, why did we end up keeping dogs, instead of foxes?

As a matter of fact, scientists in Russia *have* succeeded in domesticating red foxes, by keeping and cross-breeding them for many decades. By selecting only the 'tamest' foxes for many generations, they have produced a tame, **domesticated fox** that loves belly rubs and enjoys human company.

Unexpectedly, this selective breeding process also gave the 'tame' foxes new coat colours, curly tails and floppy, dog-like ears, which suggests that the genes for floppy ears and curly tails are linked to the ones that control 'human friendliness'.

Awesome! Can I have one?

I'm afraid not. These foxes were a one-off, and though a few were sold, the rest were turned over to zoos and animal sanctuaries. Where, hopefully, they're still getting belly-rubs today.

Top Five Facts about Foxes

1 Foxes have many cat-like features

These include eyes with vertical pupils, excellent night vision, and whiskers on their faces and wrists that help them manoeuvre around objects in darkness. Some foxes also have retractable claws for stalking and climbing.

2 Foxes are solitary

Unlike most other canids, foxes do not live in packs – preferring to hunt and sleep alone. But when raising their young, foxes do stay together in small families. A family of foxes is called a skulk.

3 Foxes are doting parents

A female fox is called a vixen. A male is called (confusingly) a dog. Both parents stay with their pups for around seven months after birth – bringing them food each day, and teaching them how to hunt.

4 Foxes are playful and intelligent

When not being hunted, red foxes have been known to form friendships with domestic cats and dogs, visiting the same house every day to frolic and wrestle. They also seem fascinated by balls – a single fox may steal hundreds of balls from golf courses each year.

5 What does the fox say? All sorts of things . . .

To call over long distances, red foxes use a high-pitched yip or bark. At closer range, male foxes argue using a strange combination of yelps and howls called gekkering, which goes *ack-ack-ack-ackawoooo-ack-ack-ack*. And during mating seasons, both male and female foxes scream to attract each other – a terrible, blood-curdling noise that sounds like a human child being tortured!

Why don't dogs climb trees?

Wolves, dogs and foxes lack the sharp, retractable claws and semi-opposable 'thumbs' of tree-climbing cats, and have less mobile shoulder and hip joints. That said, a few dogs and foxes can climb trees. And their dog-like, tree-dwelling cousins, the raccoons, are experts at it.

Really? Dogs CAN climb trees?

African wild dogs, **New Guinea singing dogs**, and **Australian dingoes** will all scramble happily up slanted tree trunks. And some domestic dog breeds are agile enough to scale chain-link fences, if they're not too high.

WHAT ARE YOU DOING UP HERE?

Since canids generally **lack** the ability to **retract their claws**, however, they quickly become **blunted**, making them useless for full-on, vertical tree-climbing.

One exception to this is the **grey fox**, which *does* have strong, hooked, retractable claws, and climbs as well as most similar-sized cats. Grey foxes can climb vertical trunks over **20 metres** tall, and make their dens in trees.

The ancestors of dogs and foxes, though, were *all* great tree-climbers.

So . . . dogs LOST the ability to climb as they evolved?

You could look at it that way, yes.

But why?

Well, with **cats**, **weasels**, **martens** and other carnivores also prowling the branches, it could be that dogs just evolved in a different direction, to fit another lifestyle. In any case, not all dog-like predators abandoned the treetops . . .

One smart, nimble-fingered family of 'tree-dogs' – the **Procyonids** – absolutely *excel* at climbing things. **Raccoons**, **ringtails** and their relatives can climb a tree better than any cat.

I know about raccoons. Don't you get them in America?

Yep. In prehistoric times, they lived in the forests of Europe, too. But those species have been extinct for millions of years, and the only ones to survive were the **red pandas** that

settled in Asia, and the **raccoons**, **ringtails**, **coatis**, **kinkajous** and **olingos** that evolved in the Americas.

Raccoons are the most common 'tree-dogs' of all. The cheeky, bandit-faced **common raccoon** is found throughout North and Central America. The sharp-clawed **crab-eating raccoon** is equally common in the swamps and forests of South America.

But the smaller, endangered **pygmy** (or **Cozumel**) **raccoon** survives only on Cozumel Island, off the eastern coast of Mexico.

Raccoons will eat whatever they can find — on the ground, or in the branches. Over the last few decades, they have also begun moving into towns and cities — knocking over dustbins to get at tasty trash, reaching through cat-flaps to steal bowls of cat food, shimmying down chimneys, opening cupboards, and helping themselves to snacks in the kitchen!

Hahaaa! A raccoon raid! That sounds hilarious!

Unless you have to clean up after them.

What about the other ones? Are they furry house-burglars, too?

Ringtails live in the dry, desert regions of the USA and

Mexico, are far smaller than raccoons and much easier to tame. Miners in the American Southwest used them to keep their draughty log cabins free of mice and rats. This earned them the name **miner's cats** (though they obviously aren't cats at all).

Coatis live in the forests of the American Southwest, Central America, and South America. Smaller than a raccoon but larger than a ringtail, the coati has a long snout, a stout body and a long, muscular tail that it holds upright when it walks on all fours. Looked at the wrong way, you could mistake it for a tiny *Brontosaurus*.

Kinkajous, **olingos** and **olinguitos** live in the forests of Central and South America, and are the smallest members of the tree-dwelling **Procyonid** family. All three are shy, nocturnal creatures, rarely seen by humans.

Kinkajous shun meat altogether, so while they are carnivores by descent, they aren't really predators at all. Instead, they dangle from branches and use their sharp teeth to break open figs, and dip their long, sticky tongues into flowers to get at the sweet nectar inside.

Olingos look very similar to kinkajous, but lack the long tongue and tail. They mostly eat figs, too, but are also known to eat insects and rodents.

The impossibly cute **olinguito** was only discovered in **2013**. Like a smaller, fluffier version of the olingo, the olinguito munches fruits and insects by night. With its round ears and tiny button-nose, it has been described as a cross between a cat and a teddy bear. Making it a strong contender for *Cutest Animal That Ever Lived*!

What are the most ferocious predators in the world, and where do they live?

Although wolves and bears have a reputation for being the scariest, the most ferocious are their smaller cousins — the **mustelids**.

The must-e-what?

Mustelids are the largest and most diverse family of dog-like carnivores. They are found all over the world — on every continent except Australia and Antarctica. In short, mustelids *rule*.

What? What are these things? What do they look like?

All mustelids have long bodies, small heads, thick necks, stubby legs and small, rounded ears. They have two layers of **fur** — a soft, dense, water-repelling **undercoat**, and a coarse, hairy **overcoat**. Like most predators, they have sharp teeth, blunted claws, long, pointed **noses**, and an excellent sense of smell.

GRRR!

Do they live in Britain?

Yep. In fact, mustelids are the most common type of wild predator in the British Isles.

Then how come I've never heard of them?

You probably have. In the UK, mustelids include **weasels**, **badgers** and **otters**. In mainland Europe, you'll find **polecats**, **martens**, and **mink**. In Africa, **zorillas** and **honey badgers**. In Asia and North America, **sables**, **skunks** and **wolverines**.

Hang on! I know badgers can be pretty mean. But weasels? Surely they're not THAT ferocious.

You'd be surprised. **Stoats**, **weasels** and **martens** generally live in forests and hunt frogs, birds and rodents. With their muscular, tube-like bodies, they bound and weave across tree branches and forest floors, crushing the skulls of frogs, birds and rodents with their powerful jaws.

The smallest of these, the **least weasel** – is the world's smallest carnivore, and also one of the most fierce! Though it measures

just **10–15 centimetres** long, and weighs just **25 grams**, the least weasel attacks things more than **ten times** its own size, including voles, rabbits and hares.

When hunting larger prey, it leaps at the throat, latching on to the carotid artery, and hanging on until the poor animal bleeds to death.

Yikes! What about the bigger ones? Are they even meaner?

The largest mustelids of all are **giant otters** and **sea otters**. **Giant otters** hunt in the rivers of South America, while **sea otters** hunt the northern Pacific Ocean.

They grow up to 1.4 metres long. But thankfully, otters are smart, playful, sociable animals that are only really dangerous to fish, crabs and shellfish.

Thank goodness!

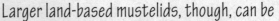

Larger land-based mustelids, though, can be ferocious beasts indeed.

The African **honey badger** gets its name from its fondness for raiding **beehives**. But this terrier-sized mustelid also hunts spiny **porcupines**, climbs into trees to kill deadly **cobras**, and has been known to attack **cheetahs** and **leopards** in the hope of stealing their kills! They're so fierce that there's an African saying that goes, 'He's tougher than a honey badger.'

The **fisher** – a stocky marten found in the forests of Canada and the northwestern USA – hunts mostly **hares** and **porcupines**. But when pressed or particularly hungry, fishers have been known to kill **bobcats**, **lynxes** and even **coyotes**.

Are they the meanest, then?

Perhaps the most fierce animal of all is the legendary **wolverine** — a small, bear-like mustelid found in Alaska, Canada, and northeastern Russia.

A scavenger and a hunter, the wolverine regularly hunts and kills wild **elk**, **mountain goats** and **wildcats**. And when defending its territory, it will attack a **bear** or **moose** over **30 times** its size.

That would be like you or me facing down a fully-grown **black rhino**. Or if you prefer, **three polar bears**.

THREE polar bears?
Err . . .
no thanks.

Many-a-Mustelid

There are more than fifty ferocious mustelid species worldwide, making them the largest and most diverse of all caniform families. Twenty are weaselled away in the grid below. How many can you spot?

BADGER
BEECHMARTEN
ERMINE
FERRET
FISHER
GIANTOTTER
HOGBADGER

HONEYBADGER
MINK
PINEMARTEN
POLECAT
SABLE
SEAMINK
SEAOTTER

SKUNK
STOAT
TAYRA
WEASEL
WOLVERINE
ZORILLA

```
M S K U N K Z O R I L L A W O E C S Y W
X L U G T M L C V C A Q R P D A X T C O
K S W I T F Q T I R K R S K A M N O J L
P D W Z K T C G I A N T O T T E R A Q V
P I N E M A R T E N F O N R B F R T A E
H D D Z A I H P P U Q A T D R R K R A R
L F U P N S F C W C Q B B I I Y W P A I
X D C F O Z E V R K X Y U B F F Q A E N
A N O V H L S L E S B D Z A Z A V Y X E
N N V R F Y E Y S M A B A D G E R E H N
X K B U C E Z C I V C B Y T J V Y R R S
R H D P C X R Z A A M X L Q D C M M F E
F D V Q I I E R I T G Q Z E R H Q I M A
P J G O Q H P X E J E T X I S M W N R M
N D D W S R Z T Y T Y O D W B B I E L I
G U K V Z B S L S E A O T T E R K N Y N
R B N B W X K H O N E Y B A D G E R K K
J R L B E E C H M A R T E N O D C I E X
P B T A Y R A K O H W D C W S Z G Y J V
E H Z F I S H E R H O G B A D G E R F Q
```

Answers on page 220

What was the largest meat-eating mammal that ever lived?

The largest meat-eating carnivore that ever lived was a prehistoric bear which stood over 3.5 metres tall and weighed over a tonne and a half! Fortunately for us, 'Arcto' has long since kicked the bucket. But some living members of the bear family aren't much smaller.

A monster-bear! Where did he live?

Arctotherium lived in South America. And although he went extinct a little over a million years ago, some of his prehistoric cousins, the **cave bears**, weighed almost as much – at around 500 kilograms. Sadly, cave bears now are all extinct, too.

Of the bears still alive today, two of the cave bear's descendants – **brown bears** and **polar bears** – are the largest. Males of either species can weigh up to 1,000 kilograms.

So where did all these huge, scary bears come from?

Bears are **caniforms**, so belong to the same, huge family as dogs, foxes, wolves, raccoons and all the other things we've looked at in this chapter.

Yeah, yeah – I know that.

Right. But there's at least one group of caniforms we haven't explored yet: the **Ursids** or **bears**.

The earliest known bear, *Ursavus*, roamed Europe, Asia and the Americas between **23** and **5 million** years ago. Small *Ursavus* species were about the size of a cat, larger ones about the size of a sheep. As they spread across the globe, these hardy little bears grew larger, became isolated in different continents, and eventually took on different shapes as they evolved.

In Asia, some grew into huge, lazy bears that shunned hunting and scavenging in favour of eating woody plants. Today, their patchy black-and-white fur makes them instantly recognizable as **giant pandas**. Despite their plant-based diet, giant pandas still weigh up to **125 kilograms** when fully grown.

In North and South America, a second group evolved known as **spectacled bears**. Largely vegetarian, spectacled bears weigh about **175 kilograms**. These dark, reddish-brown animals get their name from the light circles of fur around each eye, which makes them look like they're wearing orange specs.

Elsewhere a third group evolved into small, dog-sized *Ursus minimus* — a family of tiny 'teddy' bears that sadly didn't survive the last Ice Age. But from them came all the remaining bear species.

In Southeast Asia, these tiny teddies evolved into the small,

tropical **sun bear**, the larger, stockier **sloth bear** and the heavy-set **Asiatic black bear**.

I want to meet a sun bear. They sound cute!

They may sound cute. But although they eat more veg than meat, they are still carnivores — with claws and teeth to prove it. That said, if we're talking about *really* dangerous Ursids, it's their larger cousins you should really worry about.

American black bears grow up to two metres tall, and weigh up to **300 kilograms** — *twice* the size of pandas, and *four times* larger than sun bears. Although not

aggressive, black bear attacks in the USA and Canada happen every year — usually when a female is startled, or trying to defend its cubs. But even *they* aren't the biggest or toughest living bears.

The largest **brown bears** (also known as **grizzly bears** and **Kodiak bears**) grow up to **three metres tall**, and can weigh up to **1,000 kilograms**.

Polar bears stand a little taller than brown bears, but weigh a little less. They are found throughout the Arctic circle, although with climate change melting the ice sheets upon which they hunt and live, they are now starting to move south, where they meet both brown bears and (usually terrified) humans.

What would happen if a polar bear and a brown bear met?

That has actually happened in the wild. Usually, they fight. But sometimes, they mate and have a cub. When they, do the pale brownish offspring of a polar bear and a grizzly is called – get this – a **pizzly bear**. Bet you didn't know *that* when you woke up this morning!

Top Five Facts about Bears

1 **Bears live much longer than dogs**
Bears can live for up to 30 years in the wild. In captivity, with proper care, they can reach 40 or 50.

2 **Bears can move FAST when they want to**
Bears can reach up to 40 miles per hour at full charge – fast enough to catch a horse, and at least 10 miles per hour faster than the world's fastest human (Usain Bolt, 27 miles per hour). So don't bother trying to outrun them.

3 **Bears have good eyesight**
They see as well as humans in full colour, which is rare in mammals. This is probably to help them find coloured fruits and berries in the wild.

4 **Bears have incredible noses**
A bear's sense of smell is roughly 100 times more powerful than ours. A polar bear can smell a dead seal under a metre of solid ice!

5 **Bears are good swimmers**
All bears can swim, but polar bears are the Olympic champions. They can swim underwater, cover distances of over 200 miles without stopping, and leap 2.5 metres out of the water to surprise seals laying on ice sheets.

Do all doggies paddle?

Most canines can swim fairly well. A few cannot. But of all the doggy-paddling predators, only one truly rules the waves: the seals.

So some dogs CAN'T swim?

Right. Most can, but some can't. **Foxes** swim well enough to cross rivers and lakes. **Wolves** can swim up to eight miles, thanks to handy webbing between their toes. As for **domestic dogs**, they fall into three groups: natural, reluctant, and hopeless swimmers.

Large **dogs** like **springer spaniels** and **Irish setters** are natural swimmers. This is perhaps not surprising, given that they were bred to retrieve waterfowl during hunts.

Small hunting dogs, like **dachshunds** and **Jack Russells** generally *have* the ability to swim. But due to their shorter, stubbier legs, they are much weaker paddlers. Many small dog breeds are reluctant to jump in at first, but once they discover their paddling skills, many come to love the water!

Some dogs, however, are just not suited to paddling. **Bulldogs** and **boxers** may have trouble getting their noses above water, and tiny 'toy' dogs, like **chihuahuas** and **shih-tzus** tend to panic and lose body heat quickly in the water.

Puppies of all breeds may lack the ability to swim until they reach a certain size. Sadly, thousands of dogs drown in oceans and swimming pools every year.

That's so sad :(

Yes, it is. Though owners can help prevent this by covering pools or putting little 'dog ladders' at the edges.

So why is it wild wolves and dogs can swim, but some pet ones can't?

Wild dogs and wolves have generally kept their swimming abilities, as it helps them to survive. But some domestic dog breeds — like tiny 'toy' dogs and flat-faced pugs and bulldogs — have been shaped for other purposes, so in the absence of the *need* to swim, have simply lost the tools for doing it.

But one family of wild, dog-like predators developed in entirely the opposite direction. These salty 'sea-dogs' have **streamlined bodies**, wide, webbed **flippers** and thick **layers of fur or fat** to keep them warm.

These are the **Pinnipeds** — better known as **seals**, **sea lions** and **walruses**.

Sea lions are related to DOGS? I thought they were more like big, flippered cats. Sea. Lions. Right?

Sea lions get their name more from their predatory behaviour ('lions of the sea') rather than any relationship to felines. In fact, **seals**, **sea lions** and **walruses** are all **caniforms**.

See also lion fish, ant lions, and golden lion tamarins — which are fish, insects and monkeys, respectively.

So did the first seals look more like dogs?

Kind of, yes. The shared ancestor of all Pinnipeds was a **large, hairy, otter-like mammal** that hunted coastal seas. Unlike modern seals and sea lions, it had short, sturdy **legs**, suitable for walking on land. Its **ears** were poorly adapted for hearing underwater, so it probably used its eyes to hunt. And based on its dog-like slicing **teeth**, it probably hunted at sea, but had to drag its fishy prey back to land to eat it.

After a few million years, these dog-like creatures became adapted to full-time ocean living. Their stubby limbs withdrew into their bodies and their clawed paws turned into webbed flippers. They began to pack on flab (blubber) beneath the skin, or thick fur outside it, in order to stay warm longer in the water.

Eventually, three families of Pinnipeds emerged. The **true seals** (Phocids), the **eared seals** (Otariids), and the **walruses** (Odobenids).

How do you tell the difference?

Easy. **True seals** have no visible external ears on their smooth, rounded heads, and their hind flippers flop uselessly behind them when they move on land. They hunt mostly fish, crabs and squid, but fierce Antarctic **leopard seals** also hunt penguins, and massive **elephant seals** eat sharks and rays.

Eared seals (as the name suggests) have visible ears that stick out from their heads, and rotate their hind flippers beneath their bodies, using them to walk awkwardly on land. These include **sea lions** and **fur seals**. Both hunt fish, crabs, shrimp and squid. Some southern sea lions also hunt penguins.

Walruses live only in the northern Atlantic and Pacific Oceans, preferring to rest and give birth on the frozen ice floes of the Arctic. When hunting, male walruses use their huge tusks to scour the seabed for crabs, lobsters and clams – stirring up the silty seafloor, then sensing prey with their thick, **whiskery moustaches**.

When above the waves, males use them to **battle** each other over females – sometimes to the death. Funny and strange as they look, walruses are weighty and formidable predators. Some even hunt and eat **seals**.

A huge, seal-eating walrus?! Yikes!

Yep. That's one sea-dog I *don't* want to mess with.

Are wild dogs endangered?

While domestic dogs number in their millions, many dogs and dog-like predators are now threatened in the wild. Among them wolves, foxes, otters, sea lions and bears.

Are dogs really doing that badly?

Some are doing fine. Others, not so well. As hardy and adaptable as they are, canines and caniforms face the same problems of human poaching, encroachment and habitat destruction as do wild cats and raptors.

So which are the best and worst off?

Raccoons and **ringtails** are probably in the best shape, although one or two raccoon species, like the tiny **Cozumel raccoon**, are threatened by disappearing habitat, and live in such small areas that it wouldn't take much to finish them off.

But **common raccoon** numbers have exploded. This is probably because clever, agile raccoons have no problem at all moving into human towns – feeding on discarded rubbish and food scraps.

That doesn't sound so bad . . .

But not all caniforms are as adaptable as raccoons. Some, like **black-footed ferrets**, have gone extinct in the wild, and now survive only in zoos and sanctuaries.

Otters, **giant otters** and **sea otters** are in similarly bad shape, thanks to pollution, habitat destruction and competition from commercial fisheries.

Seals and **sea lions** face similar problems. Thanks to over-fishing and commercial hunting, many species are vulnerable to extinction.

What about foxes? Didn't we used to hunt those?

We did. Although fur-trapping and fox hunting have been banned in many places, many **wild dog** and **fox** species are still in trouble.

African wild dogs have been all but wiped out in Northern, Central and Western Africa by chicken farmers, and **Asiatic wild dogs**

(or **dholes**) have been similarly exterminated, and less than **2,500** now survive in Asia.

In South America, the rare **Darwin's fox** (discovered by the famous Charles Darwin) is down to just **320** animals. And in North America, the **Northern swift fox** and **San Joaquin kit fox** have all but disappeared, thanks to poisoning and the removal of their grassland homes to create farmland.

So is it mostly the smaller, doggie predators that are in trouble?

Unfortunately, no. Larger caniforms like **bears** and **giant pandas** are faring even worse. **Six** of the **eight** major bear species are currently listed as vulnerable or endangered.

In China, less than **1,600 giant pandas** survive in the wild, and given their reputation for slow breeding, it's unlikely they'll bounce back quickly.

Throughout Asia, **sun bear**, **sloth bear** and **Asiatic black bear** numbers have dropped by **half** during the last thirty years, mostly due to deforestation, poaching and hunting for traditional medicines.

In the far north, **20,000–25,000 polar bears** still survive on the dwindling ice sheets of the Arctic. But as climate change continues to melt the icy platforms on which they

hunt, more and more bears are venturing south to look for food. There, tourism and pollution kill as many bears as hunters, and sometimes they are shot after dangerous encounters with humans.

What about the wolves?

They're not doing too great, either. **Red wolves** and **Ethopian wolves** are already in perilously low numbers.

And some **grey wolf** subspecies have already disappeared from the world.

In all, there are fewer than **25,000** wild wolves left in Europe and Russia, and fewer than **15,000** in the USA. With numbers still dwindling worldwide, whether or not wolves will survive the twenty-first century still remains to be seen.

If we're not careful, **domestic dogs** will be all that's left of the whole wolf species, which would be a sad day for canine-kind. In fact, it would be a sad day for the Earth in general —

as removing large predators affects the natural environment in ways that are hard to predict.

Like what?

Left unchecked, deer multiply like wildfire, munching through thousands of acres of plants. When they're done with that, they wander into human towns and cities — causing road accidents and car crashes, and bringing disease-carrying **deer ticks** to our grassy lawns and gardens.

So why not just bring the wolves back?

In fact, this *has* already been tried in parts of the USA and has been suggested for the **Scottish highlands**, where in the absence of wolves, red deer now run rampant. Some ecologists have even suggested re-introducing other predators, like **bears** and **lions**, to their former habitats in

Northern Europe, Asia and America. After all — they lived there before *we* did.

Lions and bears in England? Would that work?

Hard to say. The US wolf 're-wilding' experiment has been a huge success. With wolves returned to the wild there, deer populations started to behave differently — avoiding whole areas of the park, allowing plants to regrow, changing the landscape, and providing more habitat for other animals.

That's amazing!

It is. But there are worries that trying this elsewhere – where there are more humans around – could lead to livestock predation and dangerous human–wolf encounters.

If we *can* figure out how to do it, then wolves and other predators will be granted a second chance, and allowed to return to their former glory. If not, they may dwindle to extinction as humans continue to multiply and claim their habitat.

So what should we do in the meantime?

For now, we can **keep doing research**, to find out more about the state of predator and prey species in the wild, and work out how best to protect them for the future. You also can join **organizations** – like the Defenders of Wildlife (defenders.org) or the World Wildlife Fund (wwf.org.uk) – who work to protect endangered animals and their natural habitats.

Through these, you can **adopt** a snow leopard, a tiger or a wolf and get all your friends to do the same!

And perhaps most importantly, we can all make **smarter choices** about the things we buy, so that we don't contribute to the pollution and habitat destruction that threaten predators most. Save water. Save electricity. Buy biodegradable goods and clothing. Recycle things. Make sure your fish and other foods come from sustainable sources, rather than destructive commercial fisheries, or farms built

by clearing natural predator habitat. In the end, this will do more to help predators than anything else you can do.

Who knows — with a little thought, a little work, and a little luck, we may just rebuild the natural planet. I, for one, would love to see a tiger outside my bedroom window.

As long as he doesn't pop in for tea . . .

ANSWERS

Prehistoric Puzzler (page 70)

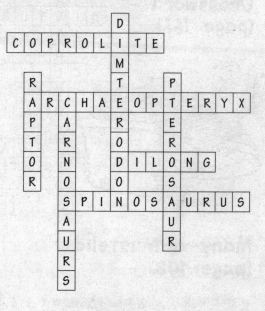

```
            D
  C O P R O L I T E
            M
  R         T         P
  A R C H A E O P T E R Y X
  P       A   R       E
  T       R   O       R
  O       N   D I L O N G
  R       O   O       S
          S P I N O S A U R U S
          A           U
          U           R
          R
          S
```

Owl Search (page 107)

```
B Z E A G L E Y L S M C V B C S V M Z V
S G B R K P E W M B A M J L N W B Q S A
R E S O N H L B Q R Z X N G S Y D C H B
E Z Y A O S W V P G K W R K Z C Q V O A
I Q M Y N B G Q T R E Y I V Z V P H R Y
C D M E J C O H E E P J C R P K Z S T O
H C X O G S Z O K A C P B S O N O N E K
Q I U F Q F X U K T H N W B N F T P A G
P R E R I Y C G H H V F R Q M V B C R E
T K B Y F J X D Q O X C V B C D P F E U
F J B D L G K F M R L J B L Z Y I D D M
B E U N D L E X C N B E V E N T B F P S
L C R U F N A X D E P A Y E Z X K E C N
H A R L F D V I N D S M R D J P L U I O
N A O B I T B C X W Q C I N K X E A E W
M M W K W L I N F I S H I N G T O I A Y
L N I K C L O Y T K M D E F Q F B O B L
V J N P B E S U M S J C U L J H J I O L
W R G I P G H K Z T A W N Y F W R A R K
B L S C O P S P A Y C A T E Q G N O I H
```

219

Feline Fancier's Crossword
(page 166)

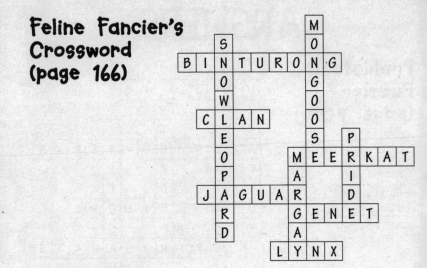

Many-a-Mustelid
(page 198)

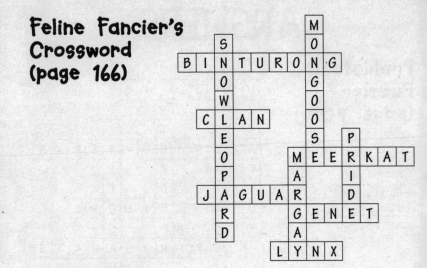